Bahamas Trilogy

Also by Sandra Riley

Homeward Bound: A History of the Bahamas to 1850

The Lucayan Taíno - First People of the Bahamas

Sisters of the Sea:
Anne Bonny and Mary Read Pirates of the Caribbean

Sometimes Towards Eden: Anne Bonny in Jamaica

Stone Poems/Wotai: Help on the Way

The Greenbear Chronicles

With Peggy C. Hall

Gus Greenbear and the Beijing Fortune Cookie Caper

BAHAMAS TRILOGY

Miss Ruby, Matt Lowe, Mariah Brown,

A COLLECTION OF HISTORICAL SOLO DRAMAS

by

SANDRA RILEY

Parrot House

2017

A Riley Hall Publication

Bahamas Trilogy: Miss Ruby, Matt Lowe, Mariah Brown, a Collection of Historical Solo Dramas

Library of Congress Cataloging-in-Publication Data is available.

ISBN#978-0-9665310-8-4

First Published January 2010
Second Printing June 2013
Third Printing December 2017

Cover painting (detail)—An original oil painting by Alton Lowe

Book & Cover Design by Frank Wendeln

Photos and Artwork by Lou Buzone, Jack Lamont, Mary Lamont, Frank Wendeln

For Luisa, Travis and Laverne who brought Ruby, Matt and Mariah to life.

And for Alton Lowe who inspired these works.

The playwright is fortunate to be able to work closely with the actor in the creation of character. It is a difficult process for any actor to assume a character and to "live" that life "truthfully under imaginary circumstances," but to do that on the stage alone takes an individual of heroic proportions. The playwright honors her heroes Luisa Black, Travis Neff and Laverne Cuzzocrea for giving audiences Miss Ruby, Matt Lowe and Mariah Brown.

Table of Contents

PRODUCTION HISTORIES

MISS RUBY

The Abaco Cultural Society (Alton Lowe, Artistic/Executive Director) produced the world premiere of *Miss Ruby* at the Lowe Gallery Stage, Green Turtle Cay, Abaco, Bahamas on May 3-5, 2001. Director - Sandra Riley; musical arrangement and piano - Peggy Hall; costume design - Marsha Kreitman; lighting design - Travis Neff.

Ruby Curry was played by Luisa Black.

MATT LOWE & MISS RUBY

The Pirates in Paradise Festival (Julie McEnroe, Festival Director) produced the world premiere of *Matt Lowe* and the South Florida premiere of *Miss Ruby* at The San Carlos Theatre, Key West, Florida on November 24-26, 2001. Director - Sandra Riley; musical arrangement and piano - Peggy Hall; costume design - Marsha Kreitman; lighting design - Travis Neff; sound design - Nathan Rausch.

Matt Lowe was played by Travis Neff
Ruby Curry was played by Luisa Black

Miss Ruby and *Matt Lowe* were further developed and produced by the Miami Light Project (Elizabeth Boone, Artistic/Executive Director; Cindy Brown, Managing Director) at the Light Box Studio Theatre, Miami, Florida on January 23-29, 2003.

MARIAH BROWN

The Crystal Parrot Players in association with the Miami Light Project produced the world premiere of *Mariah Brown* at the Ransom Everglades Pagoda, Coconut Grove, Florida on June 27-30, 2003. Director - Sandra Riley; lighting designer - Travis Neff; costume - Anna Almeida.

Mariah Brown was played by Laverne Lewis

Mariah Brown was further developed at The Woman's Club of Coconut Grove, Coconut Grove, Florida on February 18, 2004; Coconut Grove Playhouse Encore Room on May 22-23, 2004 and Vizcaya Museum, Miami, Florida on April 21-22, 2007.

The script published here made its Bahamian premiere at the Shakespeare in Paradise Festival, Nassau, Bahamas on September 30 - October 8, 2011, starring Laverne (Lewis) Cuzzocrea.

Miss Ruby

TIME AND PLACE

1927. New Plymouth, Green Turtle Cay, Abaco, Bahamas.

SET

Gillam Bay and Ruby's Porch.

CHARACTER AND COSTUME

Miss Ruby Curry (age 47) is a school teacher. She is of European and Scot-Irish ancestry. Ruby is dressed for a visitor.

Gillam Bay: Theme music plays as Ruby enters. She stands in a pool of light and breathes the morning air as the sun rises over Pelican Cay. The music stops. [Music Cue #1]

MISS RUBY: Good day, my love. I see you there in that cloud, tinged with violet, hovering over Pelican Cay. Have you followed me here to the edge of the sea? You thought I hadn't noticed you on the way. You are mistaken. I spied you everywhere, in the poinciana tree, scarlet above the yellow wall, in the bougainvillaea draped over the fence like a purple shawl. I heard you singing in the pines and whispering in the casuarinas, the music of my heart. Last evening you were the sweet fragrance of Night Jasmine and the moonlight kissing the pink hibiscus. You are the taste of mango. You're the sunshine filtering through jade waters and fishes dressed in colors artists love. The parrot fish has green teeth. Oh, I laughed when you told me that, remember? You're these jewels in the sand. All color, like my beloved Bahamas.

MISS RUBY: Darwin, a reporter from the *New York Journal* is coming to interview me. A sea plane is bringing him from Key West. Imagine that, a sea plane. He wants to know all about my life, growing up on this island, going to school in Key West. And he wants to know all about you, my love. I don't think I can talk about us. *(Listens.)* We'll see.

Lights fade and come up on Ruby's porch. Two chairs sit beside a small table, covered with a linen tablecloth on which rest a pitcher and two glasses. Ruby places her shawl over the back of the chair. She fans herself, then removes her sun hat and touches its pink ribbon. From the straw basket by her chair she takes out a bundle of letters and holds them to her heart. She removes a handkerchief from its cloth bag and looks at it as though for the first time. When she sees the reporter approaching her yard she puts the handkerchief in the pocket of her dress.

MISS RUBY: Ah, Mister Fletcher, I am so pleased to meet you. May I offer you some refreshment?

(Listens and responds to his questions as she pours.)

Miss Ruby: Yes, it is a glorious day. Oh, please call me Miss Ruby. Everybody else does.

Well, I grew up right here on Green Turtle Cay. My mother and father were born here. Their people were among the first settlers to these islands. My mother's family, the Lowes, came here way back in the 1600s. Why, they were whalers, turtlers and wreckers. Mama died when I was ten. She was beautiful. Child, that woman could cook. Best cook on the island, folks say.

(Looking out to sea.)

Miss Ruby: Look, Mr. Fletcher, there's the *Marie J. Thompson.* Largest ship ever built in the Bahamas. Launched at Harbour Island in 1922 just five years ago. "Six hundred and ninety-six tons and four masts." Daddy was a boat builder. Died last year.

(Brushes away a tear.)

Miss Ruby: Sea air makes my eyes water, but I dearly love it out here. I can look at the ocean all day and never tire of it. If you look at the ocean from dawn to dusk you can see the water turn all shades of blues, greens, even purples.

Miss Ruby: I teach at the school, right up there on that hill. Twenty-five years. Today is the first day of summer vacation or else you'd hear the ship's bell calling all the children to school. Yes, the garden is lovely, isn't it. I dearly love to garden. Daddy often told me, "Child, that's Curry blood in you, shows in that dirt under your fingernails." The Currys love the land. We crave the land almost as much as my mother's people, the Lowes, feel the pull of the sea.

(The reporter's next question brings her back to the moment.)

Miss Ruby: When I was little, growing up on this island, the Cay was prosperous. People here could always depend on the sea to feed their families, fishing for turtle and harvesting sponges. But wrecking, that was big business in the 1880s. The men worked the wrecks around Abaco and all along these cays, even the Florida Keys.

Why yes, I know a wrecking story. Did you ever hear the story about the preacher from Hope Town? Well, my mother sent me to one of those quilting parties. Women were always nattering, telling some gossip or other. Anyway, it was near the end of the service and this preacher told the people to bow their heads in prayer. "In a little while you shall see me and in a little while you shall see me no more." Well, after a respectable time, the people looked up and the preacher was gone. You see, from where the preacher was standing, he could look out to the ocean and that Sunday he saw a wreck happening on the reef. When the people looked out, they saw the preacher as he reached the wreck to claim it. *(Laughs.)* After that the people changed the pulpit. Oh yes, wrecking. Wrecking was big business for everybody.

New Plymouth was part of a trade network that included the island of Cuba, Key West and New York City. People had fine china and good crystal, even Persian rugs.

(Takes the shawl and wraps it around her shoulders.)

Miss Ruby: I remember women wearing dresses made of beautiful fabrics from Cuba, in colors of deep lavenders and capes of rich burgundy. We called them *tippets.* My mother had boots of the softest Spanish leather.

(Dances a few steps of the flamenco.)

Miss Ruby: Sunday-go-to-meeting hats we called *toques.* Small-brimmed silk hats decorated with big flowers from Havana and parasols from New York. *(Dancing.) Tippets* and *toques. Tippets* and *toques.* Tons of lace and gallons of perfume.

Which mansion? We have many two-story mansions in town with porches up and down and all around like the parsonage of the Methodist Church. That church can hold 1200 people. It has galleries, three huge swinging lamps and memorial plaques on the walls. One memorial is for Uriah Saunders, a small man with a big voice. Child, he sounded like a trumpet. He was one of the richest men in the Bahamas. So rich, the government would borrow money from him to run the country. I went to school on the porch of the parsonage.

The teacher would blow on the conch and we would come running. That's where we all learned to read. The town library had thousands of books. I read hundreds of them. I know that. I dearly love to read. When we took lunch I'd walk among the rosebud, date palms and guava trees. In school we celebrated Empire Day, still do. I remember marching into town and gathering around the flag pole, playing drums and singing songs like *(Sings.) "Rule Britannia, Britannia rules the waves." (Laughs.)*

Another? Well, let me see . . .
(Sings.)

> *We'll never let the old flag fall,*
> *For we love it best of all.*
> *We don't want to fight to show our might,*
> *But when we start, we'll fight, fight, fight.*
> *In peace or war you'll hear us sing,*
> *God save the flag, God save the King.*
> *To the end of the world, the flag unfurled,*
> *We'll never let the old . . .*

(Bringing herself back from a painful memory, she sits and fans herself.)

MISS RUBY: We had sack races and running races, sailing and model boat races. Sometimes there was entertainment in the Hall, plays like *"Barnacle Bill the Sailor Man"* and people would recite poetry they had written.

One time a Frenchman performed an act where he fought with a bear. That was scary. And a troupe of acrobats from the States walked on wires strung from the second-story veranda of one building to another porch across Parliament Street. That was scary too.

One Empire Day my schoolmate got his arm blown off trying to set off the cannon. As we carried that boy to the doctor, his dog ran off with his arm.

(Trying not to laugh.)

MISS RUBY: For months after that we made up stories to scare our friends. Since nobody knew where the dog buried that arm, we had it popping up from the ground in the cemetery, in the latrine by the jail, in the rose garden at the parsonage, anywhere and everywhere. I had nightmares about that arm for months. We were always trying to scare each other with ghost stories.

Ghost stories? Why yes, Mister Fletcher, Ethan, I know one. I heard tell people here went to bury a man, Old Pinky was his name. They put pennies on his eyes and tied up his jaw with a white cloth, put the lid on the coffin and everything. The people gathered around, like we do, throwing their hands up in the air and crying, "Oh, Lord Jesus, Pinky's gone. Pinky's done gone lef' us." The lid shot off that coffin and that man sat up, tore that cloth from his jaw and yelled, "What in thunder is this!" This is Bible.

(Sits and sips her lemonade.)

MISS RUBY: Oh, how I wish I could offer you a cool bowl of sour-sop. But they're not quite ready. Tonight maybe I'll cook up a mess of fish. Did you know I make the best Old Sour on the island. I don't know what makes it so good.

MISS RUBY: I make it the same way all the island women do. The way my mama taught me. Squeeze lemon and sour orange and put it in a medicine bottle with a bird pepper and cork it. That's what I do. Yes, tonight I'll cook up some fish with Old Sour and share it with Auntie Mizpah next door. Won't you join us Mr. Fletcher, Ethan? Good. Auntie Mizpah's been feeling poorly lately. Child, did you know I asked her how she was feeling just the other day. You know what she said? "Oh, somewhere between Oh Lord and Thank God!"

Oh! Oh! Where did this shower come from? And the sun shining so bright. See here, my flowers are laughing.

(Steps into the garden and raises her face into the rain. Darwin's theme plays.) [Music Cue #2]

MISS RUBY: Oh my, I forgot how good this feels.

(Wipes her face with her handkerchief, studies the embroidery work. The music stops.)

Miss Ruby: When I was sixteen I went to Key West to attend college. I wanted to be a teacher or a nurse. I hadn't decided which. Turned out I did both, funny how life goes. I stayed with my uncle, William Curry. He said his wife Euphemia needed help with the house. I don't wonder. The place was a mansion. But there were plenty of servants; he didn't really need my help. I think he missed his daughters since they had husbands, children and homes of their own to look after.

William Curry was the richest man in Key West. He went there from here when he was sixteen years old and not a penny to his name. Bahamians had been fishing and wrecking those waters as long as people could remember. After a while, they settled there.

Even when a hurricane caused a lumber shortage in Key West, that didn't stop two Green Turtle men from moving. Richard Roberts and John Bartlum took their houses apart, big ones too, and carried them in a two-masted schooner from Green Turtle Cay to Key West and put those houses back together again.

Those people made a fortune wrecking before the lighthouses finished that business in the Keys. Sponging and cigar making were big business when I went there in 1894.

MISS RUBY: Mr. Curry. "Rich Bill." That's what the people in Key West called my uncle. He and his sons had a ship chandlery business and tobacco warehouses and I don't know what all, invested in the stock market as well. William Curry was Florida's first millionaire, donated to many causes. He could buy anything he wanted, but he never squandered his money. You see, when he was a young man, he bought a compass and when he realized he never used it he threw it in the harbor and vowed never to buy anything useless again.

There was one purchase he made that was the envy of the world. On one of his trips to New York City Uncle Bill asked the Tiffany Company to make for him an eighteen-carat gold dinner service for twenty-four people. They made plates, cups and saucers and flatware, platters, tea and coffeepots, even salt dishes.

Mr. Tiffany displayed that set in his window and all the passers-by wanted to know, "Who is this prosperous merchant? And where is Key West anyway?" Well child, don't you know, the richest man in New York City, maybe the whole world, that's right, John Jacob Astor, saw Uncle Bill's dinner service in the window and had to own one. He asked the Tiffany Company to make him one just like it. And they did. Those are the only two dinnerware services Tiffany ever custom made. The one we used every night, and the one the Astor family used.

I attended school at the Convent of Mary Immaculate conducted by the Sisters of the Holy Name of Jesus and Mary. Reverend Mother Mary Florentine was Mother Superior and Sister Louis Gabriel came a few years later.

I studied elocution, music, painting and the languages Latin, French and Spanish. There were thousands of Cubans in Key West at that time committed to the revolution. Wealthy businessmen and the cigar manufacturers sent money to Jose Marti for their cause.

I used to love walking down Duval Street, twirling my parasol, greeting all my friends and neighbors. *"Buenos Dias." "Buenos Tardes." "Buenos No…."*

(She barely hears the reporter's question.)

MISS RUBY: What's that? Dinner parties? Why yes. The week I arrived, eight children and twenty-eight grandchildren gathered to celebrate my Uncle Bill's and Aunt Euphemia's Golden Wedding Anniversary. The newspaper wrote that the family mansion was "radiant."

Cousin Lavinia arrived from Charleston that afternoon. I sat next to her at dinner. She went on and on about the elaborate arrangements for her impending marriage. "I do declare. Lace is so expensive. Flowers are so expensive." On and on she went. I do declare this and I do declare that. Finally I said, "I hope you did declare all that stuff at the Custom's House." She didn't think that was funny. Not one bit.

Young Ruby: Lavinia, I don't think I want to get married. I just arrived and already Uncle Bill sent over a young man to meet me. He had money, but not much else. I told Aunt Euphemia, "He wants me, but I don't want him." She promptly told me, "Give him time Ruby, he may grow on you."

Lavinia: Uncle Bill's three daughters married well. I do declare, they married very well indeed. Dr. Porter, Dr. J. Vining Harris and Mr. Hellings are three of the most successful men in Key West.

Young Ruby: But just look at them Lavinia. *(Laughs.)* I figure I can go on the shelf or I could join the convent.

Miss Ruby: After dinner, there was music and Uncle Bill always asked me to sing his favorite song, *"The Last Rose of Summer."*

Miss Ruby: *(To the reporter.)*

Sing it? Now? If I can remember it.

MISS RUBY: *(Sings.)*

'Tis the last rose of summer left blooming alone
All her lovely companions are faded and gone
No flower of her kindred, no rosebud is nigh
To reflect back her blushes or give sigh for sigh.

I watched Uncle Bill take Aunt Euphemia's hand. Ever so gently, he stroked her hand. They were in love, as much in love as on their wedding day fifty years ago. Anyone could see that. If I were lucky enough to meet a man I loved like that, I'd marry him in a minute. A little more than a year later, Uncle Bill died. January 23rd 1896. *(To the reporter.)* January 23rd. I will never forget that date. I was ready to return home, but Euphemia took to her bed and I stayed on to care for her. I also tutored the younger students at the Convent School. Funny how life goes.

Back then, war with Spain had been brewing for a long time. Jose Marti was killed in battle and in June, the U.S. Battleship *Maine* made its first visit to Key West. Child, don't you know there was a smallpox epidemic and Dr. Porter wanted to erect a building to house all contagious citizens, but the city council refused. So he placed the entire city under quarantine. And the *Maine*, under orders from the Secretary of the Navy, kept all vessels without permits from leaving or entering the harbor. Just like that. Boom!

(Tries to catch her breath.)

MISS RUBY: When Dr. Porter lifted the quarantine, Key West took on the colors of summer. And on the 4th of July the officers of the *Maine* invited the townspeople to a dance aboard ship. Cousin Louisa Ann, Dr. Porter's wife, insisted I go.

(Moves her chair to mid-center.)

MISS RUBY: When she came to sit with Aunt Euphemia, she gave me a pair of white lace gloves, "Just the thing for an afternoon dance."

I flew to Government Wharf where the *Maine's* boats shuttled us to the vessel. Such a handsome ship. Such handsome sailors. The officers, in starched white uniforms and white gloves, lined the deck to greet every guest. Before I could lay my shawl over a chair, "Mess Attendant James Pinkney" asked me to dance.

(Dances.)

Miss Ruby: In fact, we kept dancing and dancing. Perspiration streamed down his face so much, I had to give him my handkerchief. He talked in the most excited way about how beautiful the town and the women of Key West were. "I hope to return here after these hostilities are over. I'd like to make Key West my home." On and on he talked until another gentleman cut in. A waltz played. I remember that.

(She dances. When the waltz music ends, Ruby sits. Music continues under their conversation.) [Music Cue #3]

Miss Ruby: Our eyes met and we spoke our names at the same instant.

Young Ruby: Ruby. Ruby Curry.

Darwin: Darwin Merritt.

Young Ruby: Darwin? I've not heard that name before.

Darwin: My father was reading Charles Darwin the night I was born. You know, the naturalist?

Young Ruby: No, I've not heard of him.

Darwin: Well, he's not an easy read. My dad may be an Iowa farmer, but he loves to read. He reads everything. He'd take me for long walks in our fields looking for bugs, noting similarities and differences between them. I'm from Red Oak, Iowa. What about you?

Young Ruby: Oh. Ruby was my great, great, great-grandmother's name. The Currys love the land too. I keep a small garden at my home in Green Turtle Cay. That's in Abaco, in the Bahamas.

Darwin: Is it as beautiful there as it is here at Key West?

Young Ruby: More beautiful.

Darwin: I don't see how. You are here. You know, Ruby, I almost didn't come this afternoon. I'm the assistant engineer of this vessel and I could not for the life of me get all the coal dust off. But the music pulled me. Besides, I had the strongest feeling that something wonderful was about to happen to me. And it has.

(Ruby dances and sings a little of "After the Ball Is Over."*)*

Miss Ruby: At 6:30 Darwin walked me to the last boat leaving for the wharf. *(Calling to him.)* *"Buenos Noches."*

Darwin and I spent some part of every day together. Whenever he could get shore leave we'd go to La Brisa to swim, dance and attend concerts. One day a sudden rain shower caught us. We lifted our faces into the rain. Then he kissed me.

Several officers had married Key West women that summer. I finally had the courage to broach the subject to Aunt Euphemia. "Absolutely not.

You've just met. We don't know anything about him. It is too soon for the two of you to even think of marriage." Cousin Louisa Ann pleaded my cause, but it was no use. Auntie was resolute.

All too soon the *Maine* received orders to leave Key West to chase filibusters running guns to Cuba. It took me the entire morning to dress for our last afternoon together. I put the pink ribbon Darwin had given me on my best hat, chose a dress to match, pulled on my lace gloves and went to meet him at the San Carlos for a piano concert.

(Sits, listens to the concert music and cries.) [Music Cue #4]

Miss Ruby: I had misplaced my handkerchief. Darwin handed me his, a beautiful one with embroidered edges. "Mother gave it to me for when I meet the right girl. She would want you to have it, Ruby. *(Beat.)* I'll write. I'll write even if there is no port to mail the letters. *Buenos Noches.*"

The months crawled by until the day cousin Elinor ran all the way from her house to tell me that the *Maine* would spend the Christmas holidays in Key West.

MISS RUBY: Even cutting through the water at 17 knots that 318 foot, coal-burning battleship couldn't get here fast enough to suit me. The first thing we did was to read each other's letters. Well, not the very first thing.

On Christmas Eve, Darwin came to escort Auntie and me to the wharf to see the battleship all lit up. Hundreds of incandescent lights ran from bow to stern, up the masts and funnel and all around the ship's sides. The *Maine* was ablaze with light. Afterward, in the Curry parlor, we had a glass of brandy to warm us. Key West was experiencing a rare cold snap. We even put on overcoats to go out that night. Darwin made a fire in the fireplace. Any Iowa farm boy knows how to do that.

He stood silent for a moment, his face glowing in the firelight. He placed a lap rug over Aunt Euphemia's knees and asked her for my hand in marriage. She said, "Please wait until after the anniversary of William's death." We set the date for January 26th.

The weather warmed, we even went swimming. We heard a gun shot from the *Maine* and knew what it meant. That was the signal for the men to return to ship. Something was wrong. That night the Captain, officers and some crewmen returned to town for the dance. We hadn't expected them to come. Darwin saw the questions in my eyes but said nothing. I saw the worried look on his face. None of the officers spoke of departure. James Pinkney said, "We'll be going to New York any day now." I knew that wasn't true.

Two weeks later on January 24th the *Maine* left Key West for the Tortugas. It was there that they received orders to proceed to Havana Harbour for a "friendly visit." Darwin and I had to say goodbye two nights before our wedding day. *"Buenos Noches, my love."*

I was sitting at Sibyl Curry's commencement ceremony in the San Carlos the night of February 15th. Sibyl had just begun to speak when the doors flew open and slammed shut. The telegraph operator found his boss in the audience and whispered into his ear the news that jumped from seat to seat. "*Maine* Blown Up! *Maine* Blown Up!" The next day angry people speculated as to the cause of the explosion. Some thought a Spanish mine, others an internal coal combustion. Oh my poor Darwin.

MISS RUBY: Key West had been the first to hear the news. I read Captain Sigsbee's cable. "*Maine* blown up in Havana Harbour and destroyed. Many wounded and doubtless more killed or drowned. All officers believed to be saved. Jenkins and Merritt not yet accounted for."

As the days and weeks passed, survivors and bodies and wreckage from the *Maine* came to Key West. Among the dead I recognized James Pinkney and I followed his body to the cemetery where he rests to this day. Mess Attendant James Pinkney had come home.

"Remember the Maine!" That's what the people were saying. The United States of America is at war with the Kingdom of Spain. School was suspended and through the herculean efforts of Mother Florentine

and Sister Gabriel the convent became a hospital in two days' time.

As Teddy Roosevelt charged up San Juan Hill, J. Vinning Harris organized a militia to defend the city. Fighting Jeptha's Home Guard they were called. After the battle of Santiago, hundreds of injured soldiers were transported from the ships in the harbor to the hospital by mule-powered streetcars. Tents had to be set up to care for the wounded.

By August the war ended and Key West celebrated. People crowded the docks to watch the Navy blow up the mines in the harbor. I stayed in my room pressing pillows against my ears, but nothing could block out the sound of those exploding mines.

I ached to go home, but Euphemia took ill. After Auntie died, I sailed home to Green Turtle Cay.

(Placing two hands at the small of her back and stretches.)

Miss Ruby: Ah life. Well.

(Ruby moves her chair back to the porch.)

MISS RUBY: Oh, yes. I kept my hope alive. I had nursed wounded soldiers with amnesia. Someday he would remember and come back to me. I met all the boats that came to this island, every one. I devoted myself to my work. I think of each child as my child and tell them the things Darwin would have told our sons and daughters. Some of my boys are so bright I can hardly wait for the others to catch up. And I tell my girls, *(Raps on her head.)* "Use your corkers. You can be anything you want to be. You can go to Nassau and keep books or be parliamentarians, chancellors even."

I tell them about Clara Barton who founded the Red Cross and Sisters Florentine and Gabriel and Susan B. Anthony who said, "Every woman should have a purse of her own." Smart women. Maybe someday women can hold important jobs and invest their own money in the stock market, like my Uncle Bill. Maybe they can do all that, marry too, and raise a family.

(Music plays.) [Music Cue #5]

MISS RUBY: I go to all the dances. I can't help myself. Something pulls me. I hear the music, put on my prettiest dress, untie my hair and fly down the street. We dance polkas and waltzes from sunset to sunrise. One time I danced so hard that in the morning I had no soles left to my shoes. The only woman who could out-dance me was Old Miss Sarah. Child, that woman could dance. Once she danced with her grandson and wore him out.

He stepped out and asked another young man to take his place and Miss Sarah wore him out too. She wore a wide skirt and held it way out and she'd dance and shout to her grandson. "Reel, Josephus, Reel!"

(Dances until she sees the sailors come in to the hall.)

MISS RUBY: One night, a group of sailors came into the dance hall. One of the older men ushered them to a section of chairs off to one side. The men in New Plymouth were jealous of the attention the sailors got from the women every time they came to town. They looked splendid in their starched white uniforms. A young man got up and came over and asked me to dance. I declined politely. As he turned and walked away I could see that the seat of his trousers was black from the coal dust the island men had placed on his chair.

MISS RUBY: It was the summer of 1912 and that morning, fifteen years ago to this very day, I received a letter from Cousin Louisa in Key West:

> It is so hard to tell you this, dear Ruby. I couldn't bring myself to write this letter for the longest time. Last March, they raised the *Maine*, recovered sixty-six bodies, which they returned to the States. They patched the hull, flew the Stars and Stripes from her masthead, towed the battleship out to sea and sank her. Sixty-five unidentified bodies were buried in Arlington National Cemetery. The only body identified was that of assistant engineer Darwin Merritt, who was taken to his hometown of Red Oak, Iowa to be buried.

(Watches the sun set.)

Miss Ruby: Look at that sunset, hanging there, all crimson, as the colors in the water take their rest.

(The lights slowly fade to black.)

MISS RUBY DIALECT NOTES

The small islands of the Bahamas are *Cays,* but the word is pronounced the same as the Florida *Keys. (All Three Plays.)*

The familiar expression, *child,* is used by Bahamians to address a person of any age. The "d" is silent and the inflection goes up at the end of the word. *"Chile!"* Miss Ruby and Mariah Brown use this expression and say it the same way.

MUSIC

Cue #1 & 2 - Page 5 and Page 14
Gillam Bay & Ruby's Garden (Darwin's Theme):
"For I Love You So"
Merry Widow Franz Lehar (1870-1948)

CUE #3 - Page 22
Maine Ball:
"Finale I," "Vilia," "For I Love You So" *Merry Widow*

CUE #4 - Page 25
Piano Concert:
"My Heart At Thy Sweet Voice," *Samson and Delilah*
Camille Saint-Saens (1835-1922)

CUE #5 - Page 31
Green Turtle Cay Dance:
"Affection Waltz" (1859),
"Kate Kearney's Waltz" (1859),
"Rory O'More Dance" (1859)

PLAY DEVELOPMENT & HISTORICAL NOTE

Alton Lowe provided the impetus for *Miss Ruby.* Bahamian artist and historian, Alton had built a museum on his much-loved island of Green Turtle Cay, Abaco. He asked me to write a play about an island woman who tells her story about growing up on Green Turtle during its heyday in the 1880s and going on to be educated in

Key West in her teens. The play and character of Miss Ruby Curry evolved from those stories and Alton's fond memories of the women in his family.

In Key West, Wright and Joan Langley shared their research material about the convent school run by the Holy Name Sisters and the Curry family. Their book *Key West & the Spanish-American War* (1998) was the inspiration for the love story between Ruby and the officer on the US Battleship *Maine.*

The frame of the play (Miss Ruby talking to the reporter) came about in development.

MISS RUBY—SYNOPSIS

Miss Ruby Curry (47) is a teacher on Green Turtle Cay, Abaco, Bahamas. The time is 1927 and a reporter from the *New York Journal* has come to the island to interview her about growing up on the small island. Ruby relives her school days, telling favorite island stories about ghosts, wrecking, Empire Day activities and island personalities. The island was prosperous in the 1880s. Salvaging wrecked vessels was big business and the town of New Plymouth, Green Turtle Cay was part of a trade network that included the island of Cuba, Key West and New York City. The best of everything could be had on the island.

Ruby goes to Key West to attend college at a convent school run by the Sisters of the Holy Name. She lives with her uncle William Curry, Florida's first millionaire. A Green Turtle Cay native, William left when he was sixteen and went to Key West to make his fortune in the wrecking business. Ruby delights in telling that every night their table was set with an eighteen-carat gold dinnerware service made by Tiffany and Company. At one dinner party, young Ruby confesses to her cousin Lavinia from Charleston that she is unimpressed with the suitors Uncle Bill has sent around to meet her. She tells Lavinia that she may have to "go on the shelf or join the convent." That is not Ruby's destiny.

Near the close of the 19th century there were thousands of Cubans in Key West who were committed to the revolution. At a dance aboard the U.S. Battleship *Maine* Ruby meets an officer and falls in love on the eve of the Spanish-American War.

Ruby discovers that telling their story is like walking in a mine field. There are emotional triggers everywhere.

Matt
LOWE

TIME & PLACE

1739. England and Spain are at war (The War of Jenkins' Ear). Beach, the Isle of Pines, Cuba.

SET

Near a broken crate partially covered with fish net is a pine branch that the actor can use as a prop, an oar or sword for example.

CHARACTER AND COSTUME

Matt Lowe (age 49) is a fisherman, wrecker and sometime pirate. He is dressed in a tattered blousy-sleeved shirt and pants cut off at mid-calf, but no shoes. He wears a zemi *(*Taíno *ornament) on a cord around his neck. A mariner's spy glass is tucked into his belt.*

Matt Lowe is lying on the beach moaning. Sound of the surf and birds. He sits up and sees an onion-shaped bottle.

MATT LOWE: Water! *(He drinks.)* Grog, and the dregs of the butt besides. *(To the audience.)* I be not drunk. You needn't think it. I were fishing, fishing along the coast of Cuba. A Spanish guard ship come upon me unawares. 'Tis plain I be a Bahamian fisherman. They board me sloop, waving their swords and shouting, *"Ingles! Ingles!"* One of their crew, his dark face burnt and scarred, seemed to know me and tells them I mean no harm. I could see 'twere no use, so I pretend to scuffle with him, forcing me purse into his hand. "Help me, friend. Samuel? *(Looks into his eyes.)* Samuel!" A blow from behind brings me down. Next thing I know, I wake in the sand, the waves slapping me feet and the sun hammering me eyelids.

(Nursing his injured head.)

MATT LOWE: Marooned. Marooned like a pirate with a bottle of rum, if you can call it that. *(Walks about the stage.)* What is this place? I should know it. I know every island, cay and rock in the Bahamas, and in the Gulf of Florida, and in the whole Caribbean Sea.

(Looks through his spy glass.)

A lagoon. Near a stand of palms. *La Isla de Pinos!* Island of Pines, Cuba. I did love a beautiful woman on this island long years ago. *(Listening.)* Even now these pines whisper our love. Yes, the sea knows too. And the birds speak of it. Hear them? Near twenty years have passed since Samuel brought me to this place. And try as I might not to think of her by day or dream of her at night, every time I close me eyes I see her standing there in a pool of flowers and all around her be a golden light, so bright as to blind me. Ana.

'Tis no punishment to leave me here alone. *(Calling out to the universe.)* You hear me. I live alone in the Bahamas on a small cay in Abaco.

'Tis a pile of rock, but this, this be paradise. I can live here with me eyes closed. *(Closes his eyes, sees her and smiles.)* Ana.

Maybe the Spanish know what I did and mean to come back to hang me up and leave me to sun dry. Or worse, roast me alive. 'Tis fitting. Times past I did commit other crimes in these waters. But this time I were only fishing. Truth is I did court me own ruin. In the deep ocean hole of sleep, I see meself all too clear. A man once say, "People don't kill banana tree. Banana tree kill theyselves." Banana ... Havana.

Bloody Jenkins. 'Tis 1739 and England be at war with Spain again. Men. We be foolish creatures. Women have more sense, that's certain. Think of it. To go to war over a man's ear. Spanish salvors were fishing one of their own wrecked treasure galleons in the Florida Keys. Captain Jenkins comes upon those divers and steals what gold they had taken up and beats away. I watched him do it for I were waiting for a chance to dive that wreck meself. I am no thief. Well, not Jenkins' kind of thief.

Matt Lowe: A Spanish guard ship catch up with Jenkins, and searching his vessel finds no plunder. That did make them mad. The Spanish captain cuts off Jenkins' ear and bid him if he finds fault with that to take it to the king. And he goes to England, mind you, presents himself to the great lords, and gives over his bloody ear as if to offer them a sweet, "I recommend me cause to me country." The sneaking puppy. To steal gold and be not man enough to take reprisal for it. And such a man as he to think himself a prince. "I recommend me cause to me country."

Where were this king when the Spanish attacked Eleuthera? Once we did settle in the Bahamas, the Spanish tried again and again to beat us off the Islands. But we be a tough-minded and hearty people, not like the gentle Indians who come afore us. I cannot abide the laws of men and ways of their kings.

Years ago, Governor Phenney said us Out Islanders be "troublesome." Belike we be living in some dark corner of the earth, so he did bring "religion and government" to Harbour Island, Eleuthera. "Nine rules: attend church, account for ships entering and leaving the harbor, muster the militia four times a year, report pirate and enemy ships to Nassau, register all wrecks, hold no land without a patent or leave the islands without written permission of the governor. Ah, no swearing or drunkenness." Patents! Me arse!

(Matt drinks.)

MATT LOWE: My friend Samuel be a sober man. But not his granddaddy, Old Pa. Growing up on Eleuthera, I had no other brother save Samuel. Our young days spent sailing, fishing, and turtling with Old Pa. Everything I know about the Bahamas I learnt from that man, all the ways of the birds and fishes, trees and plants. He learn us how to dive and how to "take de fish knife give dose conch one hit and jook out de meat."

(Sees a fish out in the ocean.)

MATT LOWE: Dolphin. Great fish, listen to me story.

Matt Lowe: You know it, you say. You do not. 'Tis a curious story. Old Pa's family were Lucayan, Taíno people, great swimmers like you fish, native to the Bahamas till the Spanish carry them off to dive for pearls at the island of Margarita. There his family mix with Africans brought to the pearl beds, as Lucayans die off from that work. One day … Fish, you listening?

One day, a Spaniard pluck Old Pa out of the sea and carries him to the Florida Keys to fish for treasure galleons wrecked on those reefs. He tells those slaves, "The first man to find a treasure ship wins his freedom." Old Pa dives down deep and spies something shiny in the sand. He ties a line to a silver bar. When they raise up that bar and read the numbers what be writ upon it, can you guess, fish? You don't know it! The name of that treasure galleon be the Margarita, the very name of the island Old Pa were born. *(Shouting to the dolphin.)* 'Tis more than coincidence! *(To himself.)* 'Tis wondrous strange.

Old Pa be of strong heart. Does he go to Cuba, a free man, and live the life of a caballero? Nay!

He sails with Bahamian wreckers to live on the islands of his people, running from the Spaniard what freed him in the first place. The whole of me life Spain and England be fighting and some Bahamian were sorry for it every time.

Mama near to losing her mind, hiding in the bush every night for fear of our lives, she begged Daddy to take us all to a place where we might live quiet and easy. Me wife, Mary Kate, were big with child. I could not decide my mind. I were a pup thinking myself a man. Mary knew my mind, yet said nought. Her parents killed by a Spaniard before her eyes, yet she were not afeard. "Think of the child, Mary Kate." "I'll not leave thee Matt Lowe, not now, not ever."

The day my family left the Bahamas, little sister followed me about crying, till I carry her to the ocean and threaten to throw her to the fishes. "Big brother, listen to me. Every day at dust dark I think of thee." They were bound for the Carolinas, from there, I know not where, for I never set eyes on them again.

MATT LOWE: We stayed along with a few others, scratching around to feed our families. Sleeping in the woods, tops of trees, sink holes. I birthed me own child in a cave. I did secretly hope for a boy, but were blessed with a sweet girl baby.

YOUNG MATT: Samuel, see here! Little Katie! Where be the old man?

SAMUEL: Fisher man come. Say Spanish attack Nassau again. Burn down everyting dis time. And dey comin' here. Old Pa take de boat, say he gonna fine dose Spaniards and let dem chase him down to Abaco. Shoutin', I free! I free! You had go bring dat old man rum.

YOUNG MATT: Old Pa need no rum to make him brave. I thank him for me wife and daughter. And I thank thee, friend.

(Hands the baby to Samuel, who oo's and ah's over her.)

SAMUEL: Your wife, Mary Kate, de brave one. Birthin' dis baby she make no sound. All de fam'lies at Eleut'ra be safe now.

MATT LOWE: We plant the baby's cord under a sour orange tree. I take me fish knife and carve the year —1706. I were sixteen years old and a husband and father. I had me a hut with no doors or windows, a driftwood table, a few broken dishes, and two spoons. Life were quiet for a time. Too quiet for the likes of me.

(Looking at the ground.)

MATT LOWE: What's this? Turtle eggs. Me lunch. *(Watching turtles hatch.)* Oh, maybe not. Look at you. Oh, gullys. Shoosh. Move off. Quit this place. Let them be. Hurry on. There you go. Dive deep! Them what are born on the beach must take to the sea. To protect my family, me an' Samuel go by turns aboard any vessel what needs crew and stay out months at a time. A Bahamian will never die from want at sea as long as he have some tackle. I can catch a shark with a noose. Rake salt at Exuma, cut cedar and pine on Abaco.

We were desperate men to carry out our lives in the face of the enemy. We did trade with Cuba and

Hispaniola in spite of the danger of capture. Any wreck cast away on some reef, we consider it our own and strip her of rigging, spars and anchors. Diving in the dark, water-filled holds to tie lines to boxes and barrels working by feel mostly. One time, my hand tangle up in a line and I near to drown before I freed myself.

MATT LOWE: Whale fishing. That were dangerous business in Bahama waters. We be fools to fix a line to a harping iron and strike a whale what would haul us into the deep or in the shoal waters drag us into the jagged rocks and coral. In a raging sea, one animal took us at lighting speed though Whale Cay Channel.

(Matt rides the waves.)

MATT LOWE: Once at the edge of the ocean, we row so close to a black whale, I did look into her dark cold eye and she into mine. Men say "the whale drink me soul," or "I have no soul, the whale have it." Nay, she took nought, rather she did turn my eye into me own soul. And for an instant I were hanging in the firmament as if pitched there by the great spray of her breath, looking down at the earth.

She dives deep and we sit in the stillness and wait, knowing not where she will breech. She could come up under us and toss us straight to heaven. I did read the movement of the sea. "Stern all for our lives!" We row mightily, her tail hanging over us like a great black cloud about to strike and shatter our boat and bones like glass. I left that business after that. 'Twere no profit in it. Sometimes at sea, I hear thee whale and listen to the whale song inside meself.

(Closes his eyes and breathes deeply.)

MATT LOWE: This island have a pleasant smell like new-ploughed earth, somewhat musky like ambergris. Sponge-like lumps, the color of ash float ashore. What be the result of a bilgy stomach to the whale were gold to me. Perfumers pay dearly for it.

Me wife and daughter love the smell of me when I come home at day's end. They hug me and kiss me. They can't get enough of me, I smell so sweet.

(Finds a coin in his pocket.)

MATT LOWE: This be a gold doubloon. The Spanish say, "Let a hermit and a thief live together, the thief would become hermit or the hermit thief." Aye, 'tis true. By the time I reached my twenty-fifth year, the Bahamas were a nursery for pirates. And Nassau be the Pirate Republic with Captain Thomas Walker always trying to meddle in their business. *(Writing.)* "I hereby p-p-petition England to p-place the Bahamas under His Majesty's government. *(Signs his name with a great flourish.)* Captain Thomas Walker, Judge of the V-V-Vice Admiralty."

That man were always writing. Pirates run him out of Nassau and he raises a battery from our few families at Harbour Island. Mounts four guns. Tells us, "Use them against the p-p-pirates, not the Spanish or the French, mind you, for we be at p-peace now." Peace. For how long? A minute. We knew the face of the enemy and 'twere not the p-pirates. Many of us be more than acquainted with pirates. We did trade with them and revel in their company.

One day, Captain Benjamin Hornigold drops anchor in our bay. He comes ashore, opens a chest and dumps a treasure of silver dishes and coin into the sand. "Be there divers among ye? We go to fish up silver from the Spanish Plate Fleet cast away in the Gulf of Florida. This be yours, me lad, and there be more, but ye must earn it." Everyday I kill myself out diving. The touch of gold sends a thrill through me sparking and fizzing like a masthead aglow with the St. Elmo's fire.

We returned to Harbour Island with a quantity of plate, coin and jewels. While Kate were in her garden, little Mary did set our driftwood table with silver bowls and cups and knives and forks, but her mother would have none of it. "I'll have no Spanish plate in my house." It did pain me to see me daughter cry. She were eight years and already a beauty like her mother.

I had dipped me hand in muddy water, as they say and 'twere now a pirate. Hornigold were captain of our pirate sloop the *Happy Return.* We took a Spanish launch what had on board over ten thousand pieces of eight. Tossed the crew overboard and bid them swim to Cuba. 'Twere not far from shore and it did them no harm to exercise. We bring that launch back to Harbour Island. Whereupon Captain Thomas Walker claps us in irons, "Befitting p-p-pirates." He writ down our names and sent that paper to the Board of Trade in Virginia! "These Eleutherans have committed p-piracies against the Spaniards on the coast of Cuba since the p-p-proclamation of the p-peace."

*(*Hornigold *takes up his sword.)*

HORNIGOLD: Walker, by what authority do ye lay hands on these men?

WALKER: My own, as J-Judge of the V-V-Vice Admiralty, Captain Hornigold.

HORNIGOLD: 'Twould be a kindness to kill thee. Ye needs killin' to mend yer speech. I warn you, Walker, if you concern yourself again, I'll burn yer house down. All the pirates at Harbour Island, Eleuthera be under my protection. Dost hear me man?"

MATT LOWE: At home, me wife call me every kind of fool to think the Spanish would suffer their money or their boat to be taken. "You have called down death and destruction upon us all." That night, she did forsake me bed and taking the gun goes to sleep in the woods. "If a Spaniard, or you, Matt Lowe, for that matter, come to me in the night, I'll blast you both to heaven."

Don't you know, the woman were right. Two months later, we learn that the Spanish did voyage out from Cuba to cut us off, men, women and children. But bad weather or bad pilots turned them home. We suffered Captain Walker to take that launch back to the Spanish governor at Havana. Samuel, having no stomach for the business of piracy did go along as crew, and stayed in Cuba. "Mary Kate, Hornigold be bound for Nassau." "If you go with him, Matt Lowe, do not bother to come back to us."

So I return to me old life. Me sloop were iron sick and the sails rotten. One day, I were trying to patch the hull when me daughter, Katie, opens me treasure chest and taking up two handfuls of gemstones she let them spill through her fingers like sand.

MATT LOWE: "Go on, dress yourself up as a pirate." Gold rings on every finger, a score of bracelets marching up each arm, a gold hoop in her ear. "Come, dance a jig with me." Ropes of pearls swinging around her neck. When she sees her mother standing there, she did drop her head onto her chest and cry. "'Tis a blessing Old Pa be not here to see this, and Samuel too. Their people spit their souls into the gold mines and pearl beds what wrought these things. Have you no shame, Matt Lowe? The rope I see tightening 'round your neck be not made of pearls, I warrant ye."

Afore I leave Harbour Island, I give little Katie a leathern pouch of silver coin and a gold cross set in rubies. "Hide these well. Tell no one, especially your proud mother. You may need them to ransom your daddy, one day."

I beat up to Nassau with me treasure. "Who's here? A stowaway. Katie? Show yourself. Katie's pet? Foolish bird. How did you get in me boat?" Ah. She put you aboard. Think I'll not come home darling girl? "Blackbird, what have a beak like a parrot, what be your business here? To save me? Hah! Look to your own safety. Flying blind. And every time you land you fall on your face. Senseless bird. Always walking into the ocean. How many times you drown, had I not saved thee? What say you to that? Oh. Look on me own folly? *(Considers this.)* Aye bird, I hear you. Save meself from meself."

Nassau be a place of many distractions. Pirates did wear their plunder 'round their necks, like me daughter. One man wore more guns and cutlasses than our entire battery at Harbour Island. Streets crowded with convicts sent out from England, rotten afore they got here, I warrant. Near two thousand souls. I did go about my business, for I did not trust myself to linger in such a place. I traded all my plate, gemstones and pearls for a good sloop, tackle and provisions. I go to the tavern to find Hornigold. He tells me of the King's Proclamation and the pardon that the new governor were bringing from England.

Matt: Will the pirates take the pardon, think you?

Hornigold: These crusty men did piss on the paper. But I be too old now to go a-piratin'. Take caution Matthew, Charles Vane be cruisin' the road 'twixt here and Harbour Island. Stay clear of him, for with the exception of Blackbeard, he be the cruelest man alive.

Matt Lowe: I know this Captain Vane for I had seen him steal away silver from the Spaniards. Aye, it shames me to say how often I did plunder the Florida wrecks. Samuel were with me the time me sloop lay becalmed in the Bay o' Biscayne two days. The water were flat an' so clear we could count the sponges. The sun baked us bone dry an' we had not a drop o' water left. A thousand eyes were watchin' us. The Florida Indian be on somewhat good terms with the Spanish, but would not abide the English. Samuel could speak a little Spanish like the Tequesta. So takin' a broken knife an' a few rusty fish hooks to trade, he rows to the Indian village at the mouth o' the river Miyami. An' he comes back with a gourd o' sweet water.

That night, we hear their drums. At a point o' land across the river from their huts, in the dim light o' the new moon we spy a circle o' moving torches. That were wondrous strange.

I set sail for home. Katie jumps into me arms. Mary has no word of greeting for me, but I did see her wipe away a tear while stirring the soup. Later I spy me daughter chattering secretly with that silly bird. Traitor.

With me family well provisioned and safe at Harbour Island, I beat down to Green Turtle to fish. That cay have good harbors to hide me sloop when I have need to go ashore for fruit. I climb a tall tree on a high hill where I can see the ocean and the harbor and spy two brigantine in the bay and a sloop wearing a black and bloody flag. 'Twere Captain Vane with his English prizes come to clean. I climb down and move closer to where a handsome lad were chipping away at the worm shells on the hull. Later I see that lad bathing in the ocean with a naked woman. When that lad did strip off his shirt, he proves to be a woman too. Women pirates. This be wondrous strange.

When I reach home, me daughter Katie runs out to the beach.

KATIE: Samuel be back from Cuba. He have a girl baby. Margarita be her name.

MATT: Margarita. *(Laughs as he takes out his pipe.)*

MATT LOWE: Samuel gives me some of his tobacco Cubano and we did sit and smoke our pipes and watch the sun fade.

SAMUEL: I see de new gov'nor roust out all de pirates, except for you, Matthew.

MATT: I be no more a pirate. I be a turtler and wrecker like me neighbors.

SAMUEL: Ah, Matt!

MATT: Samuel, I miss ye, brother.

SAMUEL: Aye. Any news of Old Hornigold?

MATT: He took the pardon. The governor sent him out after Captain Vane.

SAMUEL: I wager de gov'nor be tinkin', it do take a thief to catch a thief. *(Laughs.)* Katie done grow up a beauty.

MATT: Aye. Tell me about Margarita.

SAMUEL: She be of four years now. We live away from de people on an island of pine. But a man can't live on turtle egg, so I come here to work the fishing fleet. Come with us. Mary Kate say you too much alone. I crew your boat.

MATT LOWE: Our fleet numbered seven fishing vessels that September morning 1720. We were but two leagues from Harbour Island when a sloop wearing a black flag nearly rams us broadside. A man in calico breeches tosses me a line. Jack Rackam. The sad dog were already deep in his cups. The two women board us. I did think them brazen to announce their names for the whole fleet did hear it. Mary Read and Anne Bonny. The one as handsome as the other beautiful. Swinging a cutlass and axe, Anne Bonny orders our crew to hand over all block, tackle, line and fish.

Matt Lowe: My eyes fix upon the weapon worn by Mary Read. A Spanish sword with a gold hilt. Her sad eyes staring into empty air, like she be watching her life fall away like a fishing line slipping through her fingers. Hearing Anne Bonny ask if any man would join her crew, I were pulled into those eyes. "Nay." Mary Read did look at me. "Leave them." I could see by her look that Anne Bonny were not in the habit of having her orders contradicted. She climbs back into their sloop. Samuel tugging at my shirt to hold me back.

Mary Read did save me life that day. I soon learn Jack Rackam were hanged in chains at Jamaica. The principal evidence against him were the plunder of our fishing fleet. Anne Bonny and Mary Read did plead their bellies. 'Tis against the law to hang a woman quick with child.

I know not what become of them or their children.

Matt Lowe: *(Sings.)*

"A-rovin', a-rovin'
Since rovin's bin me ru-I-in

I'll go no more a-rovin'
With ye fair maids."

Ah, rain.

(Lifts his face into the rain and drinks, salt washes into his eyes.)

MATT LOWE: One day, watching for wrecks, the weather were foul, seas running mast high, terrible, hollow roaring of the winds, the heavens covered with sheets of lightning, and I spy an English merchantman floundering in a swell of sea. "Wreck! Wreck!" We run out in the storm waves crashing over our boats. It take the day away to bring all the passengers and crew to Harbour Island. Saving lives, that were always the first thing to be done at a wreck.

At eventide, the seas quiet and we take out our sloops to off-load cargo afore she bilge. Wrestling out boxes of indigo and bundles of tobacco. Ton after ton. Day and night without sleep. I were stone blind. I thought 'twere fatigue, but it were the water in the hold befouled with dyes and tobacco.

MATT LOWE: After three days, Samuel tells Mary Kate that he must take me to his home on the Island of Pines. "There be a old woman in Cuba what knows every plant. I'll bring him back. He'll look on thee again, I promise."

Samuel leaves me in a cave near his home where I would be safe until he comes from Havana with help. His wife put blankets on me and bid me smell a root she had crushed up, but it did not ease the pain in me head. Margarita put her little hands to me burning face and a fearful dread fills me up. If I never see again, how will I know when it be "dust dark"?

A woman come, but she were no grandmother. She gives me a tea to drink, covers my eyelids with leaves and cloth, bathes me in scented water and sings to me. She ties this *zemi* to me forehead 'twixt my eyes. Her feather touch and flower scent thrills me and I did long to look upon her face. In a palm-shaded cove she takes away the cloth. I kiss her lips. And having not the will to stand away from this reef, my weak resolve did break apart in her arms.

Our love were gentle by daylight and firelight. I knew she were royalty afore Samuel told me.

SAMUEL: She bewitch thee with her med'cines.

MATT: Rubbish.

SAMUEL: You crazy man tink you can have her.

MATT: Ana loves me.

SAMUEL: Ana come from a whole line of *Taíno* king and queen.

MATT: I love her.

SAMUEL: Tink you great *cacique*, have many wife? Tink Mary Kate go along with dat? Hah?

MATT: We can hide here.

SAMUEL: Nay. Ana be de property of de gov'nor. You 'bout to bring de whole Spanish nation down on us.

MATT LOWE: I kiss Ana one last time and carry the memory of her face in the moonlight.

I go back to Harbour Island. Home to me family. Strike turtle, fish, hunt ambergris. And though Mary Kate said she'd never leave me, one night, lying asleep in me arms, she did die. I buried her in the shade of a tall mango tree. On me daughter's wedding day, I put the ruby cross around her neck. 'Twas then that I retired to a small cay near the marshes of Abaco and lived alone, long years, till this terrible longing pulled me back to Cuba.

"Dust dark."

(After a moment Matt hears the sound of a conch.)

MATT LOWE: That be the call me and Samuel sound on the conch every time we come home to Harbour Island. *(Looks through his glass.)* A sail. That be me sloop. Ah, Samuel. That were you, brother. *(Calls out and waves.)* Samuel!

(Looks through the glass again.)

MATT LOWE: And who be this fine young gentleman hurrying along the beach ahead of you, your son?

(Laughs and looks through glass.)

MATT LOWE: That woman walking beside you? 'Tis not your wife. Matt Lowe, you dare not think it. Ana? Yes, 'tis Ana. And the lad? I see the likeness now. The lad be our son. I have a son.

Ana. Life … wondrous strange.

(Lights fade to black.)

MATT LOWE
DIALECT NOTES

The small islands of the Bahamas are Cays, but the word is pronounced the same as the Florida Keys.

The Eleutheran Adventurers came to the Bahamas by way of Bermuda in the mid-1600s. The Africans who came with them had learned English from them and the dialects mixed. The early 1700s saw the Golden Age of Piracy in the Caribbean and Nassau was the Pirate Republic of the Bahamas.

Since Matt Lowe consorted with pirates on Eleuthera and Nassau, he tends to drop the final letters of words, example: **O'** (of), **AN'** (and) and **IN'** for (ing). He alters the beginning of words. He may say **'EM** for them, **AFORE** (before), **'TIS, 'TWERE, 'TIL** or **TILL** (it is, it were, until).

Pirates usually say **CAP'N** for captain. Occasionally, depending on to whom he is speaking, Matt will substitute

YA, YE, Y', for you and **YER** for your. On occasion, **THEE** is used for you. Matt will say **ME** or **MESELF** for my and myself.

Matt substitutes **BE** for is, **WERE** for was, **WHAT** for who, **NAY** for no, **AFEARD** for afraid, **WRIT** for wrote.

Samuel and Old Pa's speech is African Bahamian. Their dialect is written in the script. Also consult Mariah Brown dialect notes page 131 of this book.

A dialect script of *Matt Lowe* is available.

MUSIC
"A-Rovin.'" *No Quarter Given Pirate Song Book.* 2nd Edition. P.O. Box 7456, Riverside, CA 92513. Copyright 1997, 2000

PLAY DEVELOPMENT & HISTORICAL NOTE

Matt Lowe was written as a companion piece to *Miss Ruby.* They can be performed on the same bill.

The play is set in 1739 during the War of Jenkins' Ear and is a stretch back into the colorful early history of the

Bahamas. In the 1640s Bermudian and Nantucket whalers fished the area and sailors from Barbados may have come north to trade. In spite of imminent attack by Spain or France, Bahamian wreckers scoured the waters of the Florida Keys, Cuba and throughout the Caribbean Sea to salvage goods for sale or trade in order to provide for their families. Men like Matt Lowe were skilled free divers and would dive for treasure in the Florida Straits. A fleet of Spanish Plate was cast away there in 1714. Pirates visited those wrecks often and made the island of New Providence their Pirate Republic about this time. But wrecking remained the chief business in the Bahamas well past Matt Lowe's time. It was dangerous and exhausting work. These men risked their lives every day diving into dark water-filled holds.

The character is fictional. However, there are documented events where the name Matt Lowe appears and fit the play's timeline, so I made them a part of the play's plot structure. A baptismal record at Eleuthera (12 July 1724) of Mary (born 1706), daughter of "Mathew and Mary Lowe" provided Matt with a family and responsibility for their care and safety. A document listing a "Matthew Low" among other Harbour Island and Eleuthera pirates involved in the hijacking of a Spanish guard ship off the coast on Cuba in 1715 bears no genealogical connection that I know of with the man in the baptism record.

But just as Matt is thrilled by diving for Spanish treasure, this pirating adventure suits his personality. I also took the liberty of placing Matt aboard the Harbour Island fishing vessel that was attacked by pirates Captain Jack Rackam, Anne Bonny and Mary Read in 1720, an event documented in their trial records.

In 1739, fishing in enemy waters along the coast of Cuba, Matt's sloop is boarded by a Spanish Guard ship. Marooned by his captors on the Isle of Pines, Matt Lowe, (age 49) reflects on his adventurous life. It is the story he might tell his son, if he had a son. Or does he?

Mariah Brown

TIME & PLACE

1903. Evangelist Street (present day Charles Avenue) Coconut Grove, Florida.

SET

Front porch and yard of the Mariah Brown House. There is an old beat-up spindle-back chair under the shade of an almond tree in the yard. A stack of books and sections of the Miami Metropolis *newspaper are next to the chair.*

CHARACTER AND COSTUME

Mariah (age 53) wears a workday shirtwaist dress. There is a crystal marble and a slim volume of poetry in the pocket of her full-length apron.

MARIAH BROWN: *(Off.)* Ooo La La!

(Mariah enters singing and dancing. She carries a small book.)

MARIAH BROWN: Ohhhh I have an auntie, an auntie Monica, and when she goes shopping, they all say Ooo La La. And so the skirt is swaying, the skirt is swaying so. And so the skirt is swaying, the skirt is sway … *(Looks at the book in her hand.)* W, weary, *(Picks up a scrap of paper from the ground.)* wasteful, *(Sees the audience.)* wonder. Upside down, M, magic, Miami. "Yes, honey. *(Listens.)* By your bed sweetheart. I coming … turec'ly. Oh, just setting out here under the almond tree enjoying the moonlight, talking with these people." *(Laughs.)* That my husband Ernest in there laughing. When a Bahamian say they do something turec'ly that could mean later in the day, next morning, next week, maybe never. M, moon, Mariah. *(Waves.)* "Evening Miss Alice. Yes, I knows, early day tomorrow. Every day early day at the Peacock Inn."

MARIAH BROWN: *(To the audience.)* Oh, I beyond grateful to the Peacocks for bed and board, to this day. But child, in the early days, I did long for a little place of my own. Every day I say, "One day Mariah, you're going to build a house of your very own." I save every penny I can. Lula say, "You're dreaming mama." But I knows I can do it. And what's more, I will read that deed, if'n it take me all night. And I will sign that paper with my very own hand. Mariah Brown.

(Writing in the air.)

MARIAH BROWN: B…r…o…w…n. *(Sings too loud.)* Glory, Glory Hallelujah! Glory, Glory Halle … Shhh, Ernest sleeping.

You want to know something. I dream me this house. Small house but it mine. And I dream me this porch running long front the house. Small porch but it mine. The big houses on the Bay like Mister Kirk and Miss Mary Munroe. Now they have a grand porch. A piazza. The Inn too, of course. Piazza. Don't ask me to write that word.

I ain't got that far in my writing. I have *(Holds up three fingers.)* tree more letters to learn and I gots them all. Oh child, that'll be some glory day.

One of those letters, zed, in the word piazza. Two time in there. I can spell good. P. Pineapple, I *(Hand on chest.)*, A. Africa, Zed, Zed, A. Africa. *(Looking at her almond tree.)* A. Almond. L. Lime. M. Mariah. O. Olivia. That's my Ella's first name but she don't use it. N. Needle. D. Dog. You say, Mariah, how come you spell so good but you can't write? Well, I tells you ... turec'ly. *(Laughs.)*

(Feels the sea breeze on her face.)

MARIAH BROWN: Vind. Truth be told I can't say the W. I shoulda did start off with some easy letter like B. Boat. Biscayne Bay. But W where I be. B. Bahamas. I from the Bahamas. North Eleut'ra. All us Eleut'rans and Abaco people, white and colored, mix up the V and the W. Not always. You see my family amongst the earliest peoples in the Bahamas, besides the Indian and the Spanish what put an end to them. Don't want to talk about that, too sad.

MARIAH BROWN: Long years past the working people from England come to Eleut'ra by way of B, Bermuda. The coloreds too, free and slave. They living so close on the sea and on the land that they pick up on each other. That the way the talk come down to us. Vind. Wh-wind. I working on that.

This almond tree grow from seed I bring with me from the Bahamas, sweetest pink seed. Child, I makes the best candy with these almonds. Cut open the seed, chop up, boil down the nuts with some sugar throw in a little coconut. Hum good! At Eleut'ra, me and Ernest sit in the shade of the almond tree looking out on the rainbow colors in the water. He read me from one of those schoolbooks, the *Royal Readers.* I never go to school.

Mama and daddy old, wore out. I grows up working: cleaning, cooking, planting, washing, same like now. We lie up against that old tree and wonder what Bermuda were like when our families live there couple hundred year ago. His free. Mine slave. The old folks always talking about Bermuda, longing for it. In the earliest days of that island, some slaves go up against the English. So the governor send them away, along with all the free Negroes to Eleut'ra. "Never to return." My great great grandaddy one of those troublesome slaves. Never to return.

Ernest and me we in love. We get to kissing, then, the urges catches us. *(Down on her knees.)* We bury twin babies under that almond tree. *(Rises.)* There we were trying to survive when a hurricane come up. Wind blow down the house, took everything. Almost take my little Ella away. Wind carry her up in the almond tree. Little feed sack dress catch on a branch and save her.

That hurricane got me to thinking. They must be more to living than this. Gots to find me some other kind of life. If'n I can't find it for myself, 'fore God I means to build a better life for my children. I tell Ernest if'n I don't starve 'fore the next fishing boat come here, I going to Key West. He say he expect it. I do believe that man know me better than I knows myself. My Ernest, he a rare man. I don't allow just any man come live in my house.

Ernest say he stay in Eleut'ra, help the people start up they gardens, then he come find me. So we go, Ella and me, with just the clothes on our backs and the pink seeds of the almond tree in my pocket.

MARIAH BROWN: All kind of people in Key West, Bahamian mostly, colored and white, doing what they been doing for hundreds of years: turtling, fishing, sponging, wrecking. I find me a house for rent on Emma Street. Eleut'rans live close and help one another. Women without their men, building a life for their children, like I doing.

I plants my almond seed, starts me a little garden and washes clothes all week. On Sundays I dresses up all fine and goes to the African Methodist Episcopal church to pray, shout and sing the praises of the Lord!
(Sings.)

I'm going to lay down my burden,
down by the riverside
down by the riverside
down by the riverside.

Mariah Brown: Mary the Washerwoman that's what they calls me. That's how I makes my living. What's more I good at it. I earn enough money to send Ella to school. There be a Jamaican man what teach the colored children in he home on Thomas Street. She go once twice, come home with her head hanging. I all excitement!

Mariah: Learn me a letter, Ella!

Ella: I can't learn my letters. It too hard.

Mariah: Learn your letters girl! Don't you want to read stories and learn things?

Ella: Mama, don't be yukin' up your vexation! Go for your walk.

Mariah Brown: *(To the audience.)* She put the iron to the clothes, moaning, "I can't. I can't." That be the saddest word I know.

I walks off my vexation. Don't take long looking at the trees. The yards crowded with bushes loaded with every kind of sweet smelling flower. All the colors: reds, yellows, oranges, purples, just a hugging the porches, falling out the fences, flaming up the trellis. My eyes full up I shuts them against the beauty. Then I cups my ears and listens to the drums: Bahamian goat skin, Cuban bongo, African *djembe.* Ernest say, "Drums too loud." That my Ernest. He come to Key West and find me like he say he would. Stay a while then go back to Eleut'ra. Come and go. Come and go. "Ernest, one these days you come this place I be gone." He say in he quiet way, "I finds you." We go on this way six seven years.

Mariah Brown: Alls I know is by the time the Peacocks reach Key West, looking for somebody to help them work the Hotel at Coconut Grove, I have tree girls. Ella, Lula and baby Alice. I tells the Peacocks I think on it. Ask them come back tomorrow. Meanwhile I talks to a man what run he boat up that way, turtling and such. He family been wrecking and fishing them waters couple hundred years, maybe more.

FISHERMAN: The Lord help you, Mariah, that Biscayne Country, wild country up there. But they's folks living on the Bay. Let me ruminate. Fort Dallas on the north side the Miami River. Coconut Grove be on the south side. At the point be William Brickell and he Trading Post. Then going on south, Pents and Frows own most that land. Jolly Jack Peacock wreck and wash ashore there. Later he send to England for he brother Charles to come and bring he family to Coconut Grove. A sailing man name of Ralph Monroe come down from New York and like the Bay so much he stay. Built heself a boat, a sharpie, he call it. He think he the first man what build a shallow draft boat. Bahamians been building those kind boats for years and years to sail around these waters. Anyway, he buy some land and ask Charles Peacock to build a hotel out of drift wood and some lumber what wash ashore from a wreck. The hotel finish and Ralph Munroe done invite he friends from way up north to stay the winter on the Bay. The Peacocks needs you, Mariah.

MARIAH: Think I should go?

FISHERMAN: If'n you wants to be et by alligator, scratch by panther, bit by rattlesnake, chased by bear then go on, go on to Coconut Grove.

MARIAH: That all? I thank you. Please tell Ernest Brown where I be.

(To the audience.)

MARIAH BROWN: That night I dreams I et by gators, scratch by panthers, bit by rattlers and chased by bears all the night long. But they no way I let my fears catch up with me. Come morning, me and my girls we pack and ready standing on the porch when the Peacocks come.

The schooner bring us into Biscayne Bay through a place call Caesar Creek. The captain frighten my girls so bad they don't sleep for a week. Talking some story about African prince carry off by slavers then shipwreck out in the ocean. "Black Caesar float into this creek an crawl up on that rock where he live. He turn pirate and do all kind bloody things. He come in the night and eat little girls in they beds!"

I tells those girls the only thing likely to eat them in they beds is the mosquitoes. Blood-sucking beastly critters!

Bahamians at Coconut Grove call theyselves 'pioneers:' Richards, Pent, Roberts, Pinder, Albury, Thompson. People with the same names in Eleut'ra and Abaco call theyselves 'just trying to survive.' By whatever name, it be a struggle, but we getting on with it. Peacocks say I to learn all the names. Bahamians taught to say Miss or Mister before any grown person Christian name. That be a sign of respect. I wants to call my employers, the Peacocks, Mister Charles and Miss Isabella. But that won't do. No woman here use the first name of a woman she talking about. Mrs. Joseph Frow. Mrs. A. R. Simmons, and she a medical doctor so they call her Dr. Mrs. Simmons. This make no sense to me. But everybody call Mrs. Charles Peacock Aunt Bella. Me too.

There be two Mr. Munroes at the Inn, Ralph Monroe and Kirk Munroe. They no relation. Child, know what the people do about they names?

They call Mr. Ralph Munroe, Commodore and he wife, Mrs. Commodore. It the longest time 'fore I learn that Mrs. Kirk Munroe name Mary just like mine.

Mariah Brown: They only two Negroes at Coconut Grove when me and my girls come here. Very soon I fetch many more from Eleut'ra, Abaco, Nassau, Key West: Alice Burrows, Dan Anderson, Nat Sampson. My Ernest find me. He the cook at the Inn. Mister Charles a good cook too. They learn from each other. The swells learn to be pioneers. The pioneers learn to be swells. I gladly do they washing if'n they plays the piano and violin, recite poetry, read stories, sing songs. We feeds them Bahamian stew fish, Seminole boil squash, English plum pudding and they feeds us culture.

All the people in Coconut Grove have a fruit patch and vegetable garden. Every settler have a coontie mill to make starch for laundry and cooking. Indian sofkee, that the best. Ernest keep a pot of that sofkee going all day: put venison, throw in there onion, rice, vegetable, sweet potato. Mister Will Brickell say he find a sweet potato fifteen foot long. Had to cut it with a saw. Can't believe a thing that man say. He blow the thing all up, paint it every color. Meats? Seminole bring bear, wild turkey and hogs. The men shoot game birds at the hunting grounds at Cutler. The sea provide turtle, manatee and all kind food fish.

Bahamians show the people how to grow in the rocks. All kind of fruit trees here now: guava, sugar apple, mango, grapefruit, Spanish lime, sapodilla, tamarind, oranges. We knows to use seaweed as mulch, put ash around young orange trees, put potato skins, table scraps around the roots of plants. We show them what fishes make the best fertilizer.

Mister Kirk love to make the yard beautiful for Miss Mary. People coming from the Bahamas bring all kind of flowering plants, hibiscus, bougainvillaea, oleander. Mister Kirk love color. The Commodore like the wildness of the hammock. He must like the mosquito too. Coconut Grove, the Commodore call it Blue Sky Country. Lots of birds in this blue sky: woodpeckers, cardinals, blue jay, little parrots, big heron on the Bay. Miss Mary Monroe dearly love the birds, snowy egret her favorite. "Save the egret!" That her mission in life. Oh, I see her snatch hats off women in the road, pull out the feathers.

MARIAH BROWN: Miss Flora love the little parrots. Almost forget her. Miss Flora McFarlane come to the Inn with the Commodore's mama. When I learn that she were a school teacher, my eyes light. And when Aunt Bella say she give her a room at the Inn to teach the children, white and colored, I fairly on fire.

You know what I going to do. My Lula just the right age for schooling and she smart. It be the quiet part of the day. Ella washing sheets. Little Alice with her. I takes Lula to Miss Flora a kicking and a screaming till I stick a piece of licorice in her mouth. Then I sets by the door and listens. Miss Flora say the letters and I say the letters along with the children. But I can't see what those letters look like.

She spell the words and I spell the words. Now you know how come I spells so good. You say, Mariah, you can't learn to read that way. Well, you right on that score.

At night I tries to get Lula to learn me the letters, but poor child she too tired. Ernest he tired too. Besides even in them early days he don't see too good especially at night. I study Lula's papers. Drawing letters on bits of old envelopes I saves from the trash and wishing I could see Miss Flora's pitchers.

One day, I outside washing. My precious papers lay out on the ground. I prays that just by looking at them, I somehow learn those letters. Don't you know a breeze come up and I has to chase down those papers. Mister Kirk come by and pick up some, but he little dog running all over them with he muddy paws. I so vex I toss those letters in the tub, watch that boiling water eat them up.

That evening Ernest say Mister Kirk want me over to he house, soon as I finish the supper dishes. "Mister Kirk say it very important you come."

MARIAH BROWN: So I go.

I cross the bridge Mister Kirk build over the creek. Seminole camp in the yard. Big Charlie probably. He always camp at Scrububs on he way to the hunting grounds at Cutler. Scrububs. Funny name for a house. Bahamians know how to name things, the Bluff, Rocky Point. Scrububs. When I reach the piazza, Wusle the dog come running and jumping up on me. "Wusle! That ain't no kind of name for a dog. Bad dog, that's your name."

Inside Miss Mary setting in a rocker. Big Charlie, he wife and children on the floor around her, cozy like. All kind of Indian things on the walls from Mister Kirk travels in the far West. Big Charlie see something and Mister Kirk take it down for him to look at. It a long blade knife. Big Charlie study that knife for a while, then he step to the middle of the room and say some Seminole words like he praying. All a sudden he stop and say thank you. Mister Kirk and Miss Mary say "Amen." I say "Ashay." I wonder why that word come out.

When the Indians go outside, Mister Kirk hand me one of my papers. It all dirty up and crinkled like it could use ironing.

(Takes the book out of her pocket.)

MARIAH BROWN: He show me a beat up old book. He done made letters with pitchers and paste them over the pages of that old book. He point to the first letter and say "A … Africa." So that's what Africa look like. *(Turns pages.)* B … Boat. H … house. P … Pineapple. On the last page … X Y Zed. "Oh, thank you Mister Kirk. May I come back sometime to see this book?" He say I welcome any time, but to take the book. He made this for me. I so 'stonished I can't talk. Miss Mary come in with tea and cakes. She put her hand on my back. I knows my back hot. You knows how it is when you cry.

I set on their porch for while. I hear Miss Mary inside rocking, singing what sound like a cradle song. A … Africa. I remembers I was about nine year old, my mama carry me to Key West to see some family. About that time the Navy take up tree slave ships and bring more then a thousand people to Key West. Oh, those people sorry looking, all skin and bones. I so afraid, I hang all over Mama's skirts thinking they ghosts.

Mariah Brown: Many get strong and go back to Africa. But some die. They bury almost tree hundred of those people somewhere on the beach. I remembers the singing and the drumming. Priest chant and we say "ashay, ashay." Mama say that word mean something like spirit moving through everything. Like we part of those people back in Africa. Part of people everywhere. In the Bahamas we say, "We's all one." That the idea back of that word. Ashay.

While we still there a woman birth a baby. All the African women gather around her and sing a song. Mama say, that the child song. Back in Africa when a woman know she have a baby inside, all the women go in the wildness with her and pray till they hear that child song. When they find it, they sing it real loud, so's the child can hear it.

The women teach the song to the whole tribe. They sing it to the baby when he born, sing it when he come a man, sing it when he marry and sing it when he die, to carry with him on to the next life. Every soul have it own song. My Ella, Lula and Alice have they songs and the two I bury under the almond tree at Eleut'ra. I still looking to hear my song. When I finds it, I'll sing it. Till then I read.

Oh yes, Mister Kirk book, a magic key unlock the door to another world. After I study this book for while I find I could read. I go around the Inn read everything: feed sacks, can goods, butter plate. *(Pantomimes turning over a plate and reads.)* "Chester Hotel China." *(Laughs.)*

I find one of those *Royal Readers* in the trash pit. It all dirty, scribble up, and smell like Wusle the dog done lift he leg on it. Hurt me to leave it. Child, the thing I find is, the more I reads and learns, the more I hurts to read and learn more. You knows that feeling too eh? When a body wants a thing so bad, they's ways. The Lord look down on us and throw us a bone from time to time.

MARIAH BROWN: Every Saturday morning, Miss Mary Munroe read to the colored children. I gets up early, do everything I think need doing at the Inn, even things don't need doing. Get Lula and Alice all clean up. Aunt Bella see me with my two girls in hand, big package of conch under my arm. She laughing. She know I going to Scrububs to hear stories.

Well, while I make the conch this and the conch that, Miss Mary read stories from a book she call *Uncle Tom's Cabin,* about Uncle Tom, Simon Legree the evil slave owner, Little Eva, Topsy. Little Alice she dance around and say, "I's wicked like Topsy." Lula hang on every word just like her mama. Lula, she name her little girl Eva and her middle boy Kirk. That my idea.

Miss Mary she tell what she call Uncle Remus stories about Br'er Bear, Br'er Fox, Br'er Rabbit. She say way Out West in the Indian stories there be a coyote, smart like that rabbit. He playing tricks on the other animals to learn them things. The characters in those stories keep going on, no matter what.

Meet up with some danger, figure a way out of that, then go on till they meet up with the next danger and so on. Just like life, especially pioneer life.

In them early days life were lonely, especially for the women folk. Come in the store for some little thing they don't need, just to hear a voice other then they children. There be one woman come around once a while her bonnet pull way down, so nobody see she crying. The Inn change all that. Like the first Christmas party. People come by boat from up Miami way, Lemon City even. Those folks a caution to watch. They never know they have so many neighbors. The Peacocks make the Inn the hub of the community. Aunt Bella everybody mama, everybody nurse, everybody friend. She build a Sunday School. Boys carry the organ over from the Inn. All the people come even Wusle the dog. Hear preaching, sing songs, eat dinner in the yard, stay all day half the night. Little time for reading on Sunday, that certain.

Mister Kirk lend me he magazines. They piles of them all over he house. Stories he writes in some of them. But I long to read news of the world so the good Lord throw me another bone. Wednesday mornings at the Inn all the men set around drinking coffee, waiting for the Commodore to get back with the news packet. What he do is sail out to the Cape on Tuesday so's he be there at the reef early Wednesday morning when the steamer come by. The Captain throw over a package of newspapers, fresh from New York City, all wrap up in canvas with a chunk a wood tied to it so it float. The Commodore he cut in there grab that packet for the canvas even get wet. *(Calling.)* "Ernest!? Hear that conch blowing? Hurry on, the Commodore like he breakfast hot."

MARIAH BROWN: Well, you think it Christmas. The men quiet for a time, eating, reading, swapping those papers. Then they get to talking. Then the talking get hot, arguing about the 'fairs of the world, how they surely solve the problems better. 'Fore they go off, they decide who gets what paper to chew on and make plans to meet later to swap again. Mister Kirk always leave behind a little piece, somewhere he knows I finds it. News of the world and I can tell just by reading my little bit of paper, this world a big place.

Coconut Grove growing. Peacock Inn spreading out. Lots of visitors down from the East. Everything growing up around me, I decides to be a part of it. Buy a little piece of land somewhere west of Mister Kirk house, if'n somebody sell me it. The women meet up at the Inn for tea from time to time to solve the problems of they worlds. I yuk up my courage and ask Mrs. Joseph Frow if'n she might sell me a piece of her land. She say yes. What's more she say I can pay for it fifty cent a week. Now, where you going buy land for fifty cent a week? That were kind of her. Settlers here always be helping each other. Child, if'n it be the same way a hundred years from now, Coconut Grove be a right fine place to live.

First thing I do is plant my almond seed so the tree be there when I get there. I plants that seed deep. Ashay. *(Points to a picture in her book.)* I finds me a carpenter, ask him to build me a house "... look just like this pitcher. And don't let me catch you using any of that old drift wood or lumber what float in off some wreck all soak in sea water. I wants Dade County pine. I don't want no critters eating up my house. I want this house built so strong it be here long after I gone. A hundred years from now, people walk by this porch and say, 'That the Mariah Brown House.'" God bless this house.

MARIAH BROWN: Couple tree years later I in my garden planting and little George Merrick come in the yard. "What you doing way over here, boy? You mama know you here?" That boy had to know everything I doing to the plants. Why this? Why that? He make me tired. He help me some, digging, pulling weeds. Then he tired, so we sits under the almond tree. I have me a half a coconut and we eats what's left inside. I take my knife, cut a little place for a stick and make a sail out of a pretty yellow-red almond leaf. "Now I wants to see you sail this boat in the bay next regatta day." *(Takes the marble from her pocket.)* He give me a clear marble and say, "Hold it up Mariah, look through it." That fairly amazing. I can see everything all around. Lots a trees and scrub. My house the only one. Well, that need remedy.

About that time, Miss Flora suggest to those women having tea at the Inn on Thursdays that they should form a club, the Housekeepers Club. They did and make Miss Flora McFarlane president. Course Miss Mary and Aunt Bella a big part of that association. Mrs. Joseph Frow too. Old settlers and new, sewing at the Post Office: baby clothes, aprons, having fairs, concerts and teas. Child, I must've made thousands of those little sandwiches. Lord knows how many cakes, pies, cookies Miss Mary make. That woman a good baker and a good talker. She get up at the meeting and say, "Women!" and go on about how they should do this and why they should do that. She never call them ladies. "Women!" They at it only a year for they build a chapel on land the Commodore give them.

Alice Burrows marry in that chapel. *(Laughs.)* On Queen's Victoria's birthday, we tease Alice all day. You see, her full name is 'Victoria' Alice. We call her 'Queen' Alice! That yuk up her vexation every time. On the day of her wedding, Miss Mary decorate the table so pretty, the Union Chapel look like a cathedral fit for a queen's coronation.

Our Queen Alice. Later, we have cake and wine at her house just down from mine. Oh yes child, we building a settlement, Nat Sampson next door, Dan Anderson and he family live down the street, houses growing up all around. Place look different in my marble now. I fetch the neighbors over to my house for tea, cakes and almond candy. We dreaming, planning ways to improve the community.

MARIAH BROWN: Cross the river, another woman dreaming in a big way. Julia Tuttle and her two children move to Fort Dallas and buy up all the land around there. Child, what that woman see in her clear marble, a entire city on the river stretching out far as she can see and more.

Well, one day they's so much excitement at the Inn, Mr. Henry Flagler and Mrs. Julia Tuttle come for dinner. You see child, the key to her plan is to talk that man in to bringing he railroad on down to Miami. Mister Charles fussing in the kitchen. Aunt Bella arranging the food on the plate. Ernest beside heself, "Aunt Bella, the food get cold, the food get cold. Mariah, throw one of them orange flowers on the plate and carry that food on out of here."

I takes up the plates, Aunt Bella fussing with my clothes as I go. That Tuttle woman be talking and talking. She see that orange blossom on the plate, smiles and keeps right on talking. When the dinner over, I serve them coffee and a little dish of my almond candy. That man take a bite and he eyes light. Most folks think it were the orange blossom Miss Julia give him, but I knows my almond candy do the trick.

'Fore long that train come in blasting it horn. Hundreds of colored people working over there, Bahamians mostly, but coloreds from Alabama, Georgia, Virginia pouring in there every day. Cracking rock, rolling roads, cutting down trees, blasting out the stumps with dynamite. Ernest nearly crazy with the noise. "Bad enough around here with Little Eunice Peacock blasting on that French horn." Funny thing you know, the blasting seem to keep the mosquito away.

MARIAH BROWN: Mrs. Tuttle give Mr. Flagler a big piece of land on the Bay to build a hotel, the Royal Palm Hotel. Clearing the land they find a hill with old bones all up in it. One of the workers tell me about that mound, how he lay out those bones careful like. Then some man what study on that kind of thing come looking at those bones and conclude that in the long long past Indian tribe bury they people there. Well, they got to take down that hill to build the Hotel. So the boss decides to put those bones in big barrels and bury them somewhere else. *(To someone in the audience.)* I don't know where! Course I trust you. I done told you about my whole life, practically. I trust you Man, that not the point. Truth be told, nobody tell me where they bury them bones.

Hear that singing? That Big Charley. Nobody tell him about moving those bones, but he know. *(Prays.)* Ashay. Ashay. That word sound like the wind. Wind touch everything. Hear that music coming from the Commodore Boathouse? He must have company.

A woman, name of Mrs. Carnegie come to the Grove in a big yacht. When she reach back home, she send Mister Kirk a box of books. Peacock & Son decide to build theyself a bigger store. And they give the top floor to Mister Kirk for a lending library. That one big fine bone the Lord throw my way.

After I finish with the supper dishes, I goes to help Mister Kirk dust the books. *(Takes one of the books off the pile.)* I think if'n I just lay my hand on these fine books I somehow soak up through my finger tips all the world's knowledge. I knows it don't work that way. When I leave for home, Mister Kirk lend me a book to read. I reading faster now. Read all night long sometimes, so's I can go back next day fetch me another book. Ernest, he say, "Woman, you going to go blind reading by that lantern."

Next couple years, things happen so fast I don't know how to tell you. Miami incorporate theyselves. The colored push the numbers over the top so's they could do it. A newspaper start up over there. Come out once a week on Fridays. Five cent. I saves pennies all week to fetch me a paper. *(Takes up one of the newspapers from under the chair and reads.)* "Ernest, paper say Key West secede from the Union again! They's trying to buy up all the Keys from the government." *(Laughs.)* Oh, listen this. "Mirrors in the palm of the glove the latest novelty. With its assistance the owner is sure her bow is at the most becoming angle." Lots a things in the paper about the Housekeepers. Those women always doing something to raise money for the community. Well, we doing the same thing.

MARIAH BROWN: The Commodore invite us to hold our fair in he yard under he coconut trees. I makes batches and batches of almond candy to sell. A dozen people crowd in my house for church till we builds one. Right here on Evangelist Street. St. Paul African Methodist Episcopal Church. Now we can sing loud as we want.
(Sings.)

Glory! Glory!
Hallelujah!
Glory! Glory!
Hallelujah!

MARIAH BROWN: Settlement growing. Mister Kirk calls it Kebo. Never learn what that Kebo mean. Maybe he make it up. Wouldn't surprise me. A man what name he house 'Scrububs' an' he dog 'Wusle,' likely to do that. What we tryin' to build here at Kebo is like climbing a mountain. We keeps going like we going we get to the top. Have a church now, then a school, maybe even a library. Dream on Mariah.

My Lula and my Alice say they going work at the Royal Palm Hotel.

LULA: Mama, they hiring lots a coloreds, waiters, maids, washerwomen. Hotel have a big dining room, 350 guest rooms and a 575 foot piazza.

MARIAH: Lula, Alice, listen to your mama. They's trouble cross the river. Bahamians not mixing too good with the coloreds from the South. I read in the paper about knifings and shootings in the Negro quarter. One woman cut her husband throat with a razor.

MARIAH BROWN: Might's well talk to these walls. I know my girls, they gots to find out things for theyselves. Right after Christmas they gone over to Miami. I suppose I could worry myself crazy. Every meeting, the Housekeepers say a Motto: "Worry kills more people than work." Anyway, they ain't no time to worry over my girls in Miami.

The tourist season come up like a waterspout. What with the new Hotel, I be thinking the Peacock Inn slow down some. That ain't the case. Swells pouring in to Coconut Grove. Inn full up. And people coming over from the Royal Palm Hotel for the day to tour the Punch Bowl and other sites. Dragging around in those heavy dresses, all full of theyselves *(To someone in the audience.)* I did, I see one woman sneak a look at her glove and give a little tilt to her hat.

A whole party set down to a meal, talking and whispering about a woman what dances on the stage name of Isadora Duncan. No Mrs. or Miss, just Isadora. "No decent woman should move her body that way. Disgraceful!" I see a young girl at the table cast her eyes down. Look like she want to dive into the fish chowder. Later I see her at the beach. She think she all alone out there, in her bare feet dancing, her body bending, stretching all kind of ways it ain't supposed to. But child, I think you don't really know a person till you knows them. Know what I mean?

One morning a young man come into breakfast after everybody gone. Sit down with a book and read while he et. By the look of that book, that man must be a scholar. All full of heself, he don't even notice me. That afternoon, I sitting on the step of the piazza, mending. That young man come up, ask me if'n I mind he set on the rocker. He have he finger in a little book. We talk about the nice breeze blowing. He say at dawn, the Bay look like liquid light. I like those words so much, I going to write them down in my book, if'n it take all night to make them look nice.

He say last night he down to the Bay enjoying the phosphorescent sea. "Why Sir, you must mean those teeny critters what sparkles they colors like little biddy stars in the water." Then he reading out loud from that little book, but I so busy sewing I think he talking.

Young Man: Have you reckoned the earth much?

Mariah: Oh yes, I watching nature all the time.

Young Man: Have you practiced so long to learn to read?

Mariah: Why yes, I …

Young Man: Have you felt so proud to get at the meaning of poems?

Mariah: How you knows that?!

Young Man: Stop this day and night with me and you shall possess the origin of all poems. You shall possess the good of the earth and sun … there are millions of suns left.

Mariah Brown: I fetches a breath, excuses myself, and leaves. Next day he gone. I didn't even catch he name. But he knew mine. Cleaning he room, I see that little book on the whatnot.

(Takes the poetry book from her pocket and reads.)

MARIAH BROWN: *Song O' Myself*—Walt Whitman. I opens it up and sees my name there in a beautiful handwriting.

"To Mariah Brown—celebrate yourself!"

Child, I reads this book so hard, I fairly wore the print off the pages. Had to look up lots of words in my dictionary. Can't find some of them. I think this Whitman fellow make up words, just like Mister Kirk. You know I done some powerful reading, but child, I ain't never read anything like this Whitman book. The words fairly eat you up. Now child don't you go telling. Nobody know I have this book. This a secret thing betwixt you and me. This my song. Your song too I expect. America's song for certain.

One night I in my garden, dancing with myself. The moon so big and bright. I stretches up my arms and "shouts my barbaric YAWP o'er the rooftops of the world." I hear Ernest fall out the bed, trip on the chair. "Mariah, where you at? Some wild animal out there, bear I think."

MARIAH BROWN: I think about that young girl dancing Isadora on the beach, me singing myself in my garden, the freedom of it! But some folks take too much freedom on theyself. Mess with things they got no business messing with. Like nature. Blasting holes in the Miami River to make it deeper, wider. I reads in the paper that they even thinking of draining off the water in the Everglades to make more land. How much land they need? Crowding the Seminole in to smaller and smaller spaces. The animals too. That just ain't right. Child, I knows I preaching. *(Puts her hand up.)* I done.

Now the turtle. I can do without venison, but my turtle steak and soup. Uh, uh! Every day over Miami, every meal practically, they serving something turtle. Ernest, he fix turtle only two time a week. Papers say turtle hunting a great sport. Tourists having egg frys on the beach under the moonlight. One day they find over nine hundred eggs. That's downright wasteful. Soon the turtle be gone. Eating up all the turtle egg that way. *(Puts her hand up.)* I done talking about this.

In Coconut Grove we watches out for nature. Mister Alfred Peacock moves the crops all around so's we always has a variety of good food at the Inn. And Mister Charles bring in all kind entertainments. Food for the soul. That man know they is more to life then eating and drinking.

One time he build a stage, decorate it, move everything around in the dining room for Mr. Gilmaine to act out little bits of Mr. Shakespeare's plays. I all excitement! You see, Mister Kirk learn me to read Shakespeare. Oh, yes! After we read together out loud two tree plays, I got so I could understand some of what they saying. I especially like Richard I, I, I.

(Each time she says "I" she places her palm on her chest).

MARIAH BROWN: Anyway, Mr. Gilmaine he strutting all about, waving he arms, chest all puff up, voice a booming. When Mister Kirk recite he Shakespeare, he don't do like that. Mr. Shakespeare turn over he grave, seeing that man do he words that way.

MARIAH BROWN: For Queen Victoria's Diamond Jubilee celebration, the Peacocks give a fancy dinner party. *(Toasts.)* "To the Queen! God bless her!" *(Sings.)*

God save our gracious Queen.
Long live our noble Queen,
God save the Queen
(Louder.)
Send her victorious, happy and glorious.
Long to reign over us.
God save our Queen.

Mister Charles, he crying. Aunt Bella she singing real loud to keep from crying. The Peacocks love this country, but they miss they home. Ernest he crying too.

Next door to my house, the Odd Fellows build them a hall. We form a Literary and Library Association and with the fifty books the Coconut Grove Library give us, we made a reading room in the Odd Fellows Hall. Mister Kirk help us set it up and promise to bring more books when he return from New England. It a good thing too because I nearly read all fifty for he reach back here.

(Brings out another copy of the paper from under the chair and scans it.)

MARIAH BROWN: I reading the newspaper to Ernest more and more. Seems he eyesight getting worse and worse. I don't tell him about all the filibustering going on to Cuba. They expecting war with Spain any day now. "Ernest, the newspaper talking about Miss Loudon's piano playing at the Housekeepers. 'The music seemed to fairly run, jump, leap and laugh from the tips of her fairy fingers as they flew, waltzed, danced and sailed over the keys.'"

(Sees something troubling in the paper.)

MARIAH BROWN: February 1898, the U. S. Battleship *Maine* get herself blow up in Havana Harbour. "America at war with Spain. Soldiers coming to

Miami from Alabama, Louisiana, Texas. Seventy-five hundred soldiers camp next to Colored Town." Seventy-five hundred soldiers with guns. I overhear a Miami merchant talking to Mister Charles, "Ignorant scum! The lot of them. Convicts released to fight a war. Help themselves to anything in the store. Terrorizing the coloreds. They're trouble." I finds trouble come mostly from people without deep seeds.

Mariah Brown: One day a company of soldiers march over to the Barnacle, right next door to the Inn. Shoot up the coconuts in the Commodore's trees. Ernest he already crazy with Miss Eunice Peacock banging on the piano now guns going off right in he ears. He think he attack by the Spanish. Had all I could do to keep that man from running off in the bush. Thank God Ella here. She fetch her husband to carry Ernest over to the house.

All tree my girls marry Williams men. Don't ask me they first names. I calls them, Williams Virginia, Williams Georgia, Williams Alabama. Lula and Alice competing to see who have they baby first.

Yeah child, they still over there, working at the Hotel, living in Colored Town. I reads in the paper that in a store full of people, a soldier see a colored man brush a white woman arm as he try to pass. Child, that soldier wait outside and shoot that man dead in the street.

In the middle the night, Lula and Alice run in the house, "Mama, Texas Company beat up a man bad and go to lynch him, but their officers stop them. Those Texas soldiers so mad at that, they come and shoot up all the kerosene lamps they see burning in Colored Town. The whole place a panic. People running every which way. We can't find our husbands."

Thank God my girls reach Coconut Grove. I keeps them safe. Alice she crying. Ernest pacing up and down, tripping over everything. Lula hold her belly and shout, "Oh, Lord, the baby coming." I tells Alice, "Go fetch Alice Burrows. Ella, send Williams Virginia for the Dr. Mrs. and watch Ernest. Don't let that man run off in the bush. He kill heself ."

MARIAH BROWN: Queen Alice here in no time. It a good thing too because the Dr. Mrs. done gone off on her horse to Lemon City. We gots to birth this baby weselves and we do. Healthy boy baby and Lula, she just fine too. "Lula, what this baby name? Don't know? Well, when he grow up and find he song, he name heself." All night I watches. Rocking this baby.

(Sings.)

Out the cradle endlessly rocking.
Endlessly rocking.

(Hums.)

Thank the good Lord the war end fast and those soldiers get on out of Miami. In September, Mrs. Julia Tuttle dead. Sudden like. I think the war doings sadden her. Maybe she troubled by what she see in her marble.

School starting. Yes child, Kebo have a school now. Every morning Johnnie Burrows hail me, running down the road with he books. Soon my grandchildren be going there. Things don't work out in Miami with those Williams men. Lula and

Alice divorce and bring they children back to Coconut Grove.

We sits on the porch and look up and down. See this girls, Mr. Stirrip building more houses cross the road, for rent. Joe Redick in one of them. Nice young man. The Counts family over there and Roberts up yonder. All this land, Frow land. They fairly give it to us. Some child in this family should bear the name Joseph or Josephine to honor that family.

Ernest, he blind now. Sets on the piazza at the Inn, staring out over the Bay. I know he see the Bahamas. As blind as he is, he know if'n he could walk on the water he go straight on out there and reach Eleut'ra. Then he wanna talk about that panther cub we raise at the Inn some year ago.

ERNEST: That cub a cute little thing. Tourists petting on him all day. Mariah, remember that man what come here to take that cub to a Zoo in New York City, Brooklyn Park? Well that panther dead in Jacksonville, Florida. All that cub want to do is live and die in he homeland.

MARIAH: Ernest, why you carrying on this way. You got gas. Let me fetch you some ginger ale for your bilgy stomach. *(Laughs.)*

MARIAH BROWN: Ernest, he not laughing. I know I must take Ernest back home where it quiet … turec'ly. The Peacocks sell the Inn. They tired. Mister Alfred try to run it for while. But he a farmer. He don't know one thing about inn keeping. Folks got to do what they do best. I still do Aunt Bella's washing, right out here under this almond tree. The Inn close down. Child, I remembers the dinner parties, dances, the joy in that house. It sad to see the old times pass. But we can celebrate the new times. I writing in a new century, whole sentences now, paragraphs even. I writing a poem.

In this house, Lula and some folks start Christ's Episcopal Church. Lula marry with Joe Redick. Nice young man. Alice marry with Jesse Brookens. Big doings in this settlement all the time. Wedding parades, Sunday suppers, Emancipation Day festivities. At one dance in the Odd Fellows hall, Lula and Alice learn us how to do the cakewalk.

Lula's Kirk and little Eva already know how to do it.

One day at our library I tell Mister Kirk I got to take Ernest back home to Eleut'ra. He say Coconut Grove will miss you, Mariah. I'll miss you. We tries not to cry.

(Sits with her book.)

Mariah Brown: I set under the almond tree to work on my poem. Ernest on the porch rocking, endlessly. "Ernest, I needs your opinion on these words. I close to finishing my poem about setting under this almond tree at night. Now tell me what better, 'the sound of laughter, the color of midnight' or 'the color of laughter, the sound of midnight.' I thank you. That it then. 'The color of laughter, the sound of midnight.'"

The day I leave, Mister Kirk bring over a box of books. He give me a pitcher of my house, put in a frame with glass. That a good thing too because it a water color and we crying all over it. "This man what I call a real artist." Mr. Kirk say, I an artist too. "Oh no Mister Kirk, you the artist, make up all those stories in your head. Your Miss Mary an artist baking all them wedding cakes. And the Commodore he boats, they beautiful to look at and fairly dance on the Bay." Mister Kirk say artists are people what can stick things together in ways that they stay stuck long after they gone, like Kebo.

MARIAH BROWN: He fetch out the box a whole set of *Royal Readers. (Picks up one of the volumes.)* He tell me this volume have the story of *Uncle Tom's Cabin.* "I has to remember this one. Number V." *(Pronounced like the letter V.)* Mister Kirk say that a Roman number, mean five. He say, I can find all the Roman numbers in my dictionary. Always some little thing to learn. Already, I see myself setting under the almond tree home at Eleut'ra reading to the children. I give Mister Kirk the last almond seed I carry from that place and the almond tree poem, written in my very own hand. I ask him please not to read it till after I gone.

"Any plays of Mr. Shakespeare in these readers?" He fetch out the box a book. *Shakespeare Complete Works.*

(Looking at the contents page.)

MARIAH BROWN: "All kind Roman numbers after these King Henry plays. Wait, don't tell me. I think I get it. The V mean five *(Holds up her palm fingers spread).* I *(Hand on chest.)* must mean one. There's Richard two, tree. So, the play I love so much be called Richard Tree." Mister Kirk say I get it. He say if'n I could take only one book with me. This be the one. This one book enough reading and thinking for a lifetime.

(Running her finger down the contents page.)

MARIAH BROWN: I think I starts with this one, Henry V.

(Like the letter V. Laughs as the lights fade to black.)

MARIAH BROWN
DIALECT NOTES

Mariah is an African Bahamian woman from Eleuthera. She speaks for all the characters in the play and for the most part, says what they say the way she would say it.

The "**TH**" sound is difficult for Bahamians. The is **DE**. The **E** is a short sound like the upside down ə in the phonetic alphabet. This, that, these, those, they, and them become **DIS, DAT, DESE, DOSE, DEY,** and **DEM**. "**D**" replaces "**TH**" at the end of some words. With becomes **WID**. Think and thank becomes **TINK** and **TANK**, three becomes **TREE**.

Many words are truncated. Usually the final consonant is dropped or changed and sometimes a vowel. For example: **AN'** (and), **TOL'** (told), **T'** (to), **YA** (you), **DAS** (that's).

Drop final consonants on words ending in **ING** and **ED.** Also, say **HE'P** for help.

Syllables before and in the middle of some words are changed or dropped entirely. Here is a short glossary:

Because ... **'CAUSE**

Before ... **'FORE**

Besides ... **'SIDES**

Coconut ... **COC'NUT**

Company ... **COMP'NY**

Directly ... **TUREC'LY**

Eleuthera ... **ELEUT'RA**

Enough ... **NUFF**

Expect ... **'SPECK**

Governor ... **GOV'NOR**

Library ... **LI'BRY**

Little ... **LI'L**

Practically ... **PRAC'LY**

Supposed ... **S'POSE**

Mariah would put these words together:

Going to ... **GONNA**

Got to ... **GOTTA**

Kind of ... **KINDA**

Might as ... **MIGHT'S**

Must have ... **MUSSA**

Out of ... **OUTTA**

Should have ... **SHOUDA**

So as ... **SO'S**

Soon as ... **SOON'S**

Want to ... **WANNA**

Pronunciation

ATTER (after)

ET (short e) (British past tense for eat)

ENT (short e) ... ain't

Can't ... **CAAN'** (the a is like ah and drawn out)

CHIL', **CHIL'REN** (one child or several)

GAS ... same as can't

Frow (Mrs. Joseph) ... **FRO**

If ... **IF'N**

Maybe ... **MEBBE**

Picture ... **PITCHER**

The familiar expression, child, is used by Bahamians to address a person of any age. The "**D**" is silent and the inflection goes up at the end of the word. "**CHILE!**"

A dialect script of Mariah Brown is available.

PLAY DEVELOPMENT & HISTORICAL NOTE

Beyond the facts that Mariah Brown came to Coconut Grove sometime in the 1880s to work at the Peacock Inn and built the first house in the African Bahamian community now called Village West, there is little information about her personal life. Miami historian, Arva Moore Parks, generously provided me with notes from interviews she held in the 1970s with residents. Kate Stirrup Dean knew Mariah's birth place and the names of Mariah's three daughters. This enabled me to find Mariah on the 1885 Key West census. With that, information provided by subsequent Coconut Grove Censuses and historical articles Arva had written on the early history of the area, I was able to write the play.

SYNOPSIS

Sometime around 1880, Mariah Brown leaves an economically impoverished Bahama island to work as a washerwoman in the thriving city of Key West to find a better life for her family. When the Peacocks ask her to work at their hotel in Coconut Grove, she moves north. Undaunted by threats of alligators, rattlesnakes, panthers and bears, Mariah labors long days at the Inn and invites her African-Bahamian friends to "yuk up" their courage and join her. From the vantage point of the hotel, the hub of the growing community, Mariah works alongside the women of the Housekeepers Club to improve the quality of life of their neighbors. She buys land and builds her own house. Other families follow suit. The African-Bahamian community establishes a church, school and library. Then the instant incorporation of the city of Miami brings social conflict, which is aggravated to a violent pitch by the arrival of soldiers preparing to fight in the Spanish-American War. Mariah can protect her family from any rattler in her garden, but this snake on her doorstep is violent and horrifying. She says, "Trouble comes mostly from people without deep seeds." She has planted deep seeds of courage, kindness and community service. The house she has built will last long after she is gone.

Parallel to the historical plot, Mariah reveals a passionate secret life in her struggle to teach herself to read and write. Her friend and mentor, Kirk Monroe, helps her by making a book of letters with pictures. Later, as she begins to read, he lends magazines and books to this woman whose hunger for knowledge is insatiable. Together they read the plays of Shakespeare aloud. When Mariah discovers Walt Whitman she states, "His words fairly eat ya up." By the end of the play she writes a poem in a Whitmanesque style and presents it to Kirk Monroe. He gives her a copy of the *Complete Works of Shakespeare* to take back to Eleuthera, Bahamas.

Throughout the play we are touched by her humor, courage and passionate joy as she breathes life into the Coconut Grove community. The voice of the African-Bahamian pioneer needs to be heard. Mariah finds her song and the time has come that we hear her sing it:

Mariah's Song by Peggy C. Hall

Have you heard how I praise this tree,
sweet almond tree?
I bless its shade, grown up from coral and
sandy earth.

I tell out loud of its sugar secrets, eaten with
stories rung far over the sea.
I sing with my tree.
But mostly, we listen, here in the dark, to the
color of laughter, the sound of midnight.

CHARACTER COSTUMES

MISS RUBY KNITTED HAT DETAIL

MISS RUBY AND MATT LOWE

Matt Lowe

MARIAH BROWN

Mariah Brown Headdress Detail
(optional)

When I took a hiatus from theater to do historical research in the Bahamas in 1973, I had no idea that I would be writing books and plays based on that work.

As Miss Ruby says, “Funny how life goes.”

Sandra Riley
January 2010

www.ingramcontent.com/pod-product-compliance
Lightning Source LLC
Chambersburg PA
CBHW051828040426
42447CB00006B/430
* 9 7 8 0 9 6 6 5 3 1 0 8 4 *